Home Office Research Study 240

A rock and a hard place: drug markets in deprived neighbourhoods

Ruth Lupton, Andrew Wilson, Tiggey May, Hamish Warburton and Paul J. Turnbull

CASE, London School of Economics and the Criminal Policy Research Unit, South Bank University

The views expressed in this report are those of the authors, not necessarily those of the Home Office (nor do they reflect Government policy)

Home Office Research, Development and Statistics Directorate
June 2002

Home Office Research Studies

The Home Office Research Studies are reports on research undertaken by or on behalf of the Home Office. They cover the range of subjects for which the Home Secretary has responsibility. Other publications produced by the Research, Development and Statistics Directorate include Findings, Statistical Bulletins and Statistical Papers.

The Research, Development and Statistics Directorate

RDS is part of the Home Office. The Home Office's purpose is to build a safe, just and tolerant society in which the rights and responsibilities of individuals, families and communities are properly balanced and the protection and security of the public are maintained.

RDS is also part of National Statistics (NS). One of the aims of NS is to inform Parliament and the citizen about the state of the nation and provide a window on the work and performance of government, allowing the impact of government policies and actions to be assessed.

Therefore –

Research Development and Statistics Directorate exists to improve policy making, decision taking and practice in support of the Home Office purpose and aims, to provide the public and Parliament with information necessary for informed debate and to publish information for future use.

Acknowledgements

The research on which this report is based was funded by the UK Anti-Drugs Co-ordination Unit (UKADCU) in the Cabinet Office and managed by the Drugs and Alcohol Research Unit in the Home Office. We are grateful for their support, particularly to Chris Goulden, Tom Bucke and Malcolm Ramsay. We would also like to thank John Graham for initiating the work and for the pilot study that he conducted.

The report is based largely on interviews with drug users, other residents including young people, and front-line staff from the police, treatment agencies and other organisations. It would not have been possible without their contributions, and we are grateful for the time they gave us and for their insights. Thanks are also due to staff in these organisations who have helped by providing background reports and statistics. Safia Noor, Mark Weaver, Tom Carter and Steve Mead helped set the report in a wider context.

Finally, we would like to acknowledge the invaluable assistance of people within our own organisations: Tim McSweeney and Jim Parsons for their fieldwork, and Professors Mike Hough and Anne Power for their guidance, expert advice and editorial work.

The Drugs and Alcohol Research Unit at the Home Office would like to thank Nigel South (Essex University) and Annette Hastings (Glasgow University) for acting as independent assessors for the report.

The authors
Ruth Lupton is a Research Officer at the Centre for Analysis of Social Exclusion (CASE) at the London School of Economics, where Dr. Andrew Wilson is a Visiting Research Associate.

Paul J. Turnbull is Deputy Director of the Criminal Policy Research Unit at South Bank University, where Tiggey May is a Research Fellow and Hamish Warburton is a Research Assistant.

The case studies are available free as a supplementary volume from CASE, via the website http://sticerd.lse.ac.uk/publications/casereports.asp or by telephoning 020 7955 6679. (full reference: Wilson, A., May, T., Warburton, H., Lupton, R. and Turnbull, P.J. (2002) *Heroin and Crack Cocaine Markets in Deprived Neighbourhoods: Seven Local Case Studies.* CASEreport 19. London, CASE.)

Foreword

This report presents the findings of a study of retail drug markets and the local action taken against them in eight deprived residential neighbourhoods in England. The work was undertaken in late 2000/early 2001 and focused mainly on markets for heroin and crack cocaine. The report concludes that it will be difficult to regenerate neighbourhoods without tackling drug markets at the same time.

Since fieldwork finished in April 2001, the Government has substantially increased the funding and guidance available to local police and Drug Action Teams to tackle these problems. In particular the Communities Against Drugs funding has been rolled out throughout England and Wales. This provides over £200m over three years to tackle these problems. It is backed by comprehensive guidance on the mapping of drug markets and the need to pay particular attention to how these operate in the most deprived areas, much as is recommended by this report.

Furthermore, resources released through the Government's comprehensive spending review have ensured that funding for treatment and young people has substantially increased since the researchers undertook the fieldwork. The respective formulae for the allocation of each of these resources have ensured that these funds are partly targeted on the basis of deprivation, with the aim that in these neighbourhoods and others like them, substantial changes will have taken place since the report fieldwork was completed.

DAVID PYLE
Head of Drugs and Alcohol Research Unit
Research, Development and Statistics Directorate
Home Office
2002

Contents

Summary

This report presents the findings of a study of retail drug markets in deprived residential neighbourhoods, undertaken in late 2000/early 2001.

The aims of the study were as follows:

- To identify the extent of drug market activity in such neighbourhoods and to describe its nature and scale.

- To draw out any associations between types of area and types of drug market.

- To understand how drug market activity affects disadvantaged neighbourhoods.

- To find out how local agencies and local communities, singly and jointly, are tackling drug markets and with what effect.

The report aims to look at neighbourhood drug markets in the context of the new policy agenda for neighbourhood renewal, including the Neighbourhood Renewal Strategy, Neighbourhood Renewal Fund, New Deal for Communities and neighbourhood management arrangements.

It covers eight neighbourhoods of varying type, tenure, location and ethnic mix, and in six different regions of England. In each neighbourhood, we interviewed front-line staff and residents who were knowledgeable either about the detail of the drug market, its impact on the area (if any) or the broader problems of the area and the responses being taken. We also interviewed a small number of drug users (between six and nine) in each area, and collected supporting documents and statistics. We focused on markets for heroin and crack cocaine.

All the markets considered could be described as vibrant and busy. Heroin was easily available in all markets and crack in six of the eight. The availability and use of both drugs was reported to be increasing, with crack increasing more rapidly from a lower base.

The cost of drugs was consistent across markets. However, cheaper drugs at dealer levels coupled with increased availability were leading to falling street prices and changes in selling practices enabling better deals. Established divisions in the sale of different drugs (primarily heroin and crack) were also being eroded, with an increase in the level of violence and use of firearms. In most neighbourhood markets, sellers and buyers were increasingly involved in violent incidents.

Selling structures varied between markets. Smaller markets were often controlled by a handful of suppliers, supplying a number of middle level sellers who worked with a number of small-scale sellers and runners. These markets were primarily closed, i.e. purchases were only possible where buyers were known to sellers. Deals were arranged via mobile telephone and drop-off points (mainly street-based locations) were arranged. Three areas had open markets alongside closed ones. Open markets are those that buyers can access directly. Selling structures in these neighbourhoods appeared to be more fluid and responsive to changes in market conditions.

The markets could be divided into two broad types, which were found in different types of areas. The first type were long-established with wide reputations, drew buyers from outside the area, had open as well as closed selling and were vulnerable to competition. We found these in inner city areas, with mixed housing type and tenure, significant transient populations, and mixed ethnicity. The second type had less widespread reputations, served buyers mainly from the local area and had closed selling with established buyer/seller arrangements. We found these in outer city areas with stable populations that were almost exclusively white and culturally homogenous. Some markets did not fit completely into one type or another, but shared some characteristics of each.

The impact of drug markets in deprived neighbourhoods is variable, giving rise to the need for local strategies based on local information. It also seems to be changing. The decline of open selling, with more and more deals conducted by mobile phone, is reducing nuisance associated with particular sites. Discarded needles are still a concern in some areas, in localised pockets, but in others appear to be less prevalent than they were. While some neighbourhood impacts are decreasing, certain areas with drug markets are experiencing increasing levels of violence. Extreme violence is found particularly in large, central place markets with contested distribution systems and buyers and sellers from outside the area as well as within it. In these areas, residents can be acutely fearful for their personal safety, resulting in unwillingness to contribute evidence or get involved in activities that may help resolve the problems.

In all of these areas, the drug market was one of a number of neighbourhood problems, not on their own a sufficient condition for neighbourhood decline or depopulation. However, where markets had become established, they were an impediment to regeneration, damaging community confidence and adding to the poor reputation of the area. Moreover, the market for crack, in particular, was providing a significant economic opportunity for young people whose formal labour market prospects were weak. It will be difficult to regenerate neighbourhoods without tackling drug markets.

While there was evidence of effective practice, the responses of local agencies, in sum, were not adequate given the scale of the problem. There was an absence of co-ordinated multi-agency strategies at local level. Partnerships that could be in a position to deliver such strategies had insufficient information with which to work. Drug Action Teams (DATs) appeared to lack the organisational capacity to operate at neighbourhood level and regeneration partnerships had not generally adopted a strategic role in relation to drug markets.

The report recommends that, in New Deal for Communities (NDC) areas, regeneration partnerships should be required to review drug market activity and develop co-ordinated strategies, incorporating enforcement measures, to develop community confidence in addressing the problem, treatment services and education and prevention strategies. DATs have a role to play in supporting the development of such strategies, and in initiating similar strategies in areas without NDC partnerships. They should be made accountable for the development of neighbourhood drugs strategies, and should be adequately resourced to fulfil this function. We also suggest that there are genuine resource problems hindering effective local action against drug markets. To inform future policy, we need better knowledge about required resource levels, and the additional return that could be expected from higher levels of investment at local level. The report proposes that pilot sites for the development of local drugs strategies are identified, properly resourced and fully evaluated.

Finally, we acknowledge that effective action against heroin and crack will not be resolved by interventions only at local level. It requires adequate resourcing at national and international level as well as critical thinking about appropriate and differentiated strategies for dealing with the different challenges of heroin and crack. This report reveals a complex and growing problem that requires a concerted and co-ordinated response at all levels.

1   Introduction

Drug markets: the neighbourhood dimension

This report presents the findings of a study of retail drug markets in deprived residential neighbourhoods, undertaken in late 2000/early 2001. It covers eight neighbourhoods of varying type, tenure, location and ethnic mix, and in six different regions of England, describing the level and nature of drug market activity, its impact on the neighbourhood, and the action being taken to tackle it and its consequences.

This broad snapshot adds to a growing body of knowledge about how drug dealing is organised (Eck, 1995; Natarajan et al., 1995; Edmunds et al., 1996; Dorn et al., 1992; Dorn et al., 1998; May et al., 1999 & 2000) and about specific strategies to combat it. These include:

- policing strategies (May et al., 2000; Jacobson, 1999; Edmunds et al., 1996; Lee, 1996; Murji, 1998; Newburn and Elliot, 1998; Wright et al., 1993; Chatterton et al., 1998)

- supply reduction through controlling importation of drugs (Ruggiero and South, 1995; Dorn et al., 1992)

- demand reduction through treatment programmes (Edmunds et al. 1998 & 1999; Turnbull et al., 2000)

- demand reduction through education programmes (Newburn and Elliot, 1998; DfEE, 1998; Home Office, 1999; Hurry and Lloyd, 1997)

- multi-agency and community-based approaches to drug prevention and enforcement (Howard et al., 1993; Henderson, 1995)

Few of these studies have looked at drug markets in their local context: examining how they affect the residential neighbourhoods in which they are situated, and how local agencies and local communities attempt to control drug market activity. No major UK study since the late 1980s (Dorn et al., 1987; Parker et al., 1988) has adopted this focus. Our report looks specifically at this neighbourhood dimension, one which is particularly important at the current time, as new government policies for neighbourhood management and regeneration begin to be implemented. While these policies represent a new opportunity to get to grips with the drug problem, there are also concerns that their wider impact on neighbourhood conditions and economic and social problems could be limited by vibrant drug markets that draw young people away from legitimate opportunities and cause crime, nuisance, fear and intimidation.

The impact of drug markets on neighbourhoods

That drug markets have a negative impact on the (mainly deprived) neighbourhoods in which they are situated is recognised by the Government in its ten-year drugs strategy, 'Tackling Drugs to Build a Better Britain', launched in 1998. The main emphasis is on the impact of drug-related crime. Indeed, one of the four main aims of the strategy is to protect communities from drug-related anti-social and criminal behaviour.

"drugs are a very serious problem in the UK…a threat to health, a threat on the streets and a serious threat to communities because of drug related crime." (ibid., p.1)

Interviews we conducted with residents and police in twelve deprived neighbourhoods around England and Wales in 1999 (Lupton, 2001) confirmed that drug-related crime, anti-social behaviour, intimidation and violence were among the most common and worrying problems for residents in these areas. There were other problems too: disturbance from people visiting dealing sites, discarded needles, fear of drug users behaving unpredictably or in a threatening fashion, and concerns about the involvement or potential involvement of young people as users or dealers. These problems have also emerged from other neighbourhood studies (e.g. Page, 2000; Wood and Vamplew, 1999), and from a brief study of three neighbourhoods that we conducted in 2000 as a prelude to the development of the current research (Graham, 2000). The work undertaken at CASE suggested that while use of cannabis, tranquillisers and stimulants (including amphetamines, ecstasy and powder cocaine) was widespread, neighbourhood problems were mainly associated with markets for heroin and crack. The problems associated with the markets were, in each case, seen as a hindrance to the creation of a safe, amenable environment. They were a day-to-day management problem. In extreme cases, and where housing supply significantly exceeded demand, they were also a major contributory factor to rapid neighbourhood depopulation and a barrier to repopulation by people who had any housing choice, countering the efforts of regeneration programmes to stabilise population and rebuild confidence (Lupton, 2001; Graham, 2000).

Moreover, the problem did not seem to be diminishing. Drug use in these neighbourhoods was perceived (by police and residents) to be increasing, a view supported by broader surveys, which have reported increasing heroin and crack use, particularly among the poor (Parker *et al.*, 1998; Ramsay and Partridge, 1998; Plant and Miller, 2000; Bennett, 2000). The trade in illegal drugs appeared to go on largely uninterrupted by police or by other agencies. Similarly ineffective interventions were reported by May *et al.* in 2000.

New policies for deprived neighbourhoods

At the same time as the problems associated with the local trade in heroin and crack appeared to grow, deprived neighbourhoods began to benefit from new mechanisms and resources for their day-to-day management and longer-term regeneration, culminating in the National Strategy for Neighbourhood Renewal (January 2001) and the establishment of a central government Neighbourhood Renewal Unit. Compared with its predecessors, the current government has both targeted more money at the poorest neighbourhoods and developed a more comprehensive approach to tackling their problems. Previous governments have relied principally on short-life centrally-funded regeneration programmes (such as the Single Regeneration Budget and City Challenge). The current government has a similar programme, the New Deal for Communities, with a longer timescale, more community involvement and broader scope. But it is also directing more money towards mainstream services in deprived neighbourhoods through the Neighbourhood Renewal Fund, and changing the way in which neighbourhood problems will be tackled. Local authorities will need to have Neighbourhood Renewal Strategies to access this funding, and Local Strategic Partnerships to co-ordinate plans and service delivery, and there will be targets, set nationally, to close the gap between the poorest neighbourhoods and the rest. Many neighbourhoods where social and economic problems are concentrated will be locally managed, with services co-ordinated through a neighbourhood manager, and will have neighbourhood wardens to enforce social order and keep a check on the quality of the local environment. There are also other area-based programmes dealing with specific issues, such as Health Action Zones, that can also be expected to bring new funding and new approaches to tackling the problems of the poorest neighbourhoods. Appendix 1 outlines these initiatives. Together, they present a powerful new opportunity to improve both short-term conditions and long-term prospects.

Specific mechanisms are also in place to address local drugs problems through multi-agency working. Drug Action Teams (DATs) were set up in 1995 with a remit to assess the nature and scale of local drug problems and the effectiveness of responses, to ensure local action in line with national drugs strategy, and to bring together the policies and operations of local agencies. They are strategic bodies with representation at senior level from the police, local authority, health authority, probation and prison service, but with Drug Reference Groups (DRGs), comprising representatives of community-level organisations (such as treatment services, youth services and housing organisations) to provide advice and information, a forum for exchange of information, and a link to the local community. Local Crime and Disorder Reduction Partnerships (CDRPs) established under the Crime and Disorder Act 1998 also have a role to play. Indeed, the 'Communities Against Drugs Initiative', announced in April 2001, gave £220 million to CDRPs over the next three years, to tackle drug-related crime in high crime areas with significant drug problems. Suggested strategies include visible policing, supporting neighbourhood wardens, and support for community and parents' groups. The aim is to focus on local priorities with local partnerships deciding how the money should be spent.

Aims of the study

It was in the light of this new policy agenda that our study was framed. We aimed to help neighbourhood managers, regeneration professionals, members of DATs and CDRPs, and policy-makers at national level to better understand the current dynamics of drug markets and their implications for deprived neighbourhoods.

We had four specific aims:

- To identify the extent of drug market activity in such neighbourhoods and to describe its nature and scale.

- To draw out any associations between types of area and types of drug market.

- To understand how drug market activity affects disadvantaged neighbourhoods.

- To find out how local agencies and local communities, singly and jointly, are tackling drug markets and with what effect.

It is also worth emphasising here what we have not set out to do – to evaluate specific interventions for demand reduction, treatment or enforcement. Other studies, including those referenced on page one, are doing this detailed work. Nor have we set out to provide a blueprint for tackling neighbourhood drugs problems. We see our work as a contribution to the development of more co-ordinated, informed and effective responses, which must ultimately be developed locally. Chapter 7 provides some pointers as to how that might be done.

A selection of deprived neighbourhoods

The study is based on a sample of deprived neighbourhoods in England. Given the six-month timetable for the project, we were limited to eight sites. For practical reasons, we were also limited to places known to the research team, where contacts had already been established and where the work could be carried out quickly. We were, however, concerned to ensure that the study was based on a diverse range of neighbourhoods, in different parts of the country and in different physical, economic and cultural settings. We therefore began by identifying areas known to the team. Eleven were identified. Using data for the electoral wards most closely corresponding to these areas, we then confirmed that they were among the ten per cent most deprived in the country, using the Index of Multiple Deprivation (IMD) (DETR, 2000)[1]. The IMD is now the most widely used measure of area deprivation, based on six domains of deprivation: income, employment, health and disability, education, skills and training, housing and access to services, measured at ward level. We then selected eight of the eleven to match our sample as closely as possible to the overall distribution of the poorest neighbourhoods in terms of region, tenure and ethnicity, using 1991 Census data. With the exception that no coalfields or areas of rural deprivation were included, this match was achieved.

Although the development of the sample was based on ward data, wards mean very little to the average person (Glennerster *et al.*, 1998), and are not necessarily synonymous with neighbourhoods. 'Neighbourhood' is a nebulous concept, with no strict definition. Indeed, as Dorn *et al.* (1987) recognised in their study on identifying neighbourhood heroin problems,

"any theoretically derived definition is likely to face difficulties when faced with the variety of social forms to be found in a society which is diverse in terms of region, ethnicity, social class, tradition and culture." (ibid., p.6)

There is broad agreement that neighbourhoods are relatively small, "made up of several thousand people" (Social Exclusion Unit 2000) and that they are identifiable by people who live there, "delineated ... within physical boundaries where people identify their home and where they live out and organise their private lives" (Power and Bergin, 1999: p.9). We adopted these

---

1   The IMD is based on wards. Where the areas we knew were not wholly contained within one ward, we used the ward covering the greatest part of the area.

broad conceptualisations. For each place in our study, we arrived at a definition of neighbourhood based on the understanding of local people, determined by natural or man-made boundaries, housing type or tenure, socio-economic or ethnic mix, history, or a combination of all of these factors. Some of the neighbourhoods we chose were large social housing estates or collections of smaller estates. Others were inner city areas with mixed housing type and tenure. One was a small town. None was more than about a mile and a half across and their populations ranged between about ten and about 20 thousand people[2]. We do not claim these as definitive definitions of these neighbourhoods. It could certainly be argued that they contain smaller neighbourhoods within them, defined differently for different purposes and by different people. They are, nevertheless, reasonable working boundaries with which local people could identify. We describe the neighbourhoods briefly in Table 1.1. To avoid creating or consolidating reputations for these areas as ones where drugs are available, we have given them false names, and to avoid repetition, we have also used the term 'area' synonymously with 'neighbourhood'.

Six of the eight neighbourhoods were known to the research team only as deprived neighbourhoods, not as drug markets. We were aware that there was some local concern about illicit drugs in five of these, but not of its extent. It was certainly possible that this concern could have related to widespread drug use, rather than to the existence of a localised market where drugs were bought and sold. Only two sites were known to us from previous drug market research. In other words, we did not deliberately select neighbourhoods that we knew to have vibrant drug markets. Our report records drug market activity and responses to it across a fairly representative selection of deprived neighbourhoods, not across a selection of known drug markets. In this light, its findings are telling.

---

2   The neighbourhoods tended to cross electoral ward boundaries or be contained within them, so it is difficult to obtain up-to-date population estimates. We have based these estimates on rough calculations using 1998 ward population estimates, or on data supplied by regeneration programmes with boundaries matching our neighbourhoods.

Table 1.1: Description of the neighbourhoods

Neighbourhood	Description
Seaview	An inner city area, with mixed housing type and tenure. A majority white area with a significant African-Caribbean minority.
Bankside	An inner city area, with predominantly privately owned and rented homes and a majority of Asian (mainly Pakistani) residents.
Riverlands	An inner city area. Council houses developed in the 1960s and 1970s are the predominant housing type. A majority white area with a significant African-Caribbean minority.
Hilltop	An inner city area with mixed housing types but council housing the majority tenure. A majority white area with significant Asian (mainly Pakistani) and African-Caribbean minorities.
East-Docks	An inner city area, mainly made up of post-war council houses and flats. A majority white area but becoming increasingly ethnically mixed, with a significant black African minority among others.
Kirkside East	An outer city neighbourhood, dominated by council estates. Almost exclusively white population.
Overtown	An area just outside a major city. Dominated by council estates. Almost exclusively white population.
Beachville	A seaside town, comprising mixed housing types and tenures, including an area of former hotels now operating as bed and breakfast hostels. Almost exclusively white but with a growing refugee population.

Neighbourhoods and their drug markets

Within each neighbourhood, the study has concentrated on the drug market – i.e. the buying and selling of illegal drugs – rather than patterns of drug use as such, simply because it is the drug market activity that is typically problematic for the neighbourhood as a whole, rather than for individuals and households. In common with other studies (Edmunds et al., 1996; May et al., 2000) we focused on markets for heroin and crack cocaine.

Markets are not synonymous with neighbourhoods. Heroin and crack selling takes place within neighbourhoods, not throughout them. It is concentrated in smaller pockets, and can be displaced around the neighbourhood by enforcement activity, by the arrival or departure of sellers, or by the adoption of different selling practices. Its impact tends to be felt much more in certain parts of a neighbourhood than others, such that residents may have differing perspectives on its extent and impact, depending not just on their individual characteristics and social networks but on their location and travel patterns. Moreover, the 'fit' between drug markets and neighbourhoods is a variable one. In some markets, both buyers and sellers are local people, whereas some markets attract buyers from outside and others attract sellers. These issues are explored in later chapters.

Methodology

The study covered eight sites in five months from December 2000 to April 2001. We used a rapid appraisal method (Beebe, 1995), comprising semi-structured interviews with knowledgeable local people (professionals and residents), supported by the collection of selected, readily available statistics and documents. Interview schedules for police and drug users were adapted from those used in a recent and more detailed study of two drug markets by members of the research team based at South Bank University (May *et al.*, 2000). Interview schedules for other informants were adapted from an exploratory study in three other sites in early 2000, by members of the research team based at LSE (Graham, 2000).

In each site in the current study we interviewed front-line staff and residents who were knowledgeable either about the detail of the drug market, its impact on the area (if any) or the broader problems of the area and the responses being taken. Figure 1.1 lists typical informants in an area, although there was inevitable variation arising from the different structures of organisations, the presence or otherwise of different agencies and the availability of individuals for interview. Residents were interviewed via a variety of mechanisms: in some cases in organised groups gathered together by workers on our behalf, and in some cases by informal contact on the street or in public amenities (such as libraries and youth clubs). We attempted to achieve a mix of residents of different ages, ethnic backgrounds and levels of involvement in neighbourhood affairs, but these attempts were necessarily partial given the time allowed. We do not claim to have represented all perspectives or carried out a community survey, although in some cases we were also able to draw on such documents as further evidence.

Between 28 and 60 staff and residents were interviewed in each area. Appendix 2 gives a detailed breakdown.

Figure 1.1:   Typical respondents

Housing manager

Supported housing/resettlement project/hostel manager

Police sector inspector

Local police constable/sergeant(s)

Drugs squad or force intelligence squad officer(s)

DAT co-ordinator

Drug treatment agency worker(s)

Needle exchange/drug prevention project worker(s)

Youth Offending Team worker(s)

GP

Youth worker(s)

Community worker(s)

Probation representative

Employment Service/New Deal manager

Regeneration project manager/neighbourhood manager

Religious leader

Workers in other relevant local voluntary organisations (e.g. youth/health)

Local councillor(s)

Residents (groups or individuals)

Young people (groups or individuals)

Drug users (individuals)

Dorn *et al.*'s study (1987) on the identification of neighbourhood heroin problems demonstrated that it was easier for lay people and others to identify major increases in drug use than minor fluctuations, and also that users and dealers often had the most valuable information about local patterns of use and dealing. Thus, in addition to staff and resident interviews, we also interviewed a small number of drug users (between six and nine) in each area, including only people who bought or sold drugs locally and who were using heroin or crack, or both. We consider this to be the minimum number of user interviews with which to build (in conjunction with other perspectives) a view of the local drug market. The timescale for this project did not allow us to interview more. Larger samples might usefully be considered in future research.

In total we interviewed 55 users, 37 men and 18 women. The youngest user was aged 18 and the oldest 50, and their median age was 30. Only in one area (Kirkside East) were we able to interview a group of users who were appreciably younger (average 21 years). Thirty-eight of the users had lived in the area for ten years or more, and only four had been there a year or less, so the sample overall consisted of people who were very familiar with their areas as well as their drug markets. There was only one area, Riverlands, where a majority of users had not been in the area for ten years or more.

The majority of the users were using drugs on a daily basis. Thirty-eight of those who supplied detailed information about their current drug use were users of both heroin (or methadone) and crack. There were 11 who used heroin (or methadone) but not crack, most of them in two areas, Beachville and Kirkside East. Only three of the crack users were not also using heroin or methadone.

Table 1.2: **Profile of drug users**

	Number of users	Number living in area for 10 years or more	Number of users of heroin/ Methadone but not crack	Number of users of crack but not heroin/ Methadone	Number of dual heroin/ Methadone and crack users
Seaview	7	6	1	1	3
Bankside	6	4	1	0	5
Riverlands	9	2	1	0	8
Hilltop	6	6	0	0	6
East-Docks	9	5	0	1	7
Kirkside East	6	6	5	0	1
Overtown	6	5	0	1	5
Beachville	6	4	3	0	3
TOTAL	55	38	11	3	38

Note: Three of the users were not currently using or did not supply information about their drug use.

The users were offered £20 for their participation in the study. In three sites, they were initially contacted through drug agencies or in some cases were known to the research team from previous work. Further contacts 'snowballed' from these. In five sites, the users were mainly recruited by face-to-face contact. The researcher observed local street activity and handed out flyers inviting people to participate in the study. 'Snowballing' took place from these initial contacts as well. In all sites, care was taken to avoid being drawn exclusively into a small network of users with a particular perspective, on occasion turning down potential respondents recommended by existing contacts in favour of making fresh contacts. Drug use and involvement in the local market had to be confirmed before agreeing to the interview. We told users (and other respondents) that the aim of the project was to examine links between drug markets and area deprivation and provided a brief outline of the project when requested.

Methodological issues will be more fully explored in a forthcoming paper. For this purpose, it is worth bearing in mind that the aim of the sampling was not to obtain a representative sample of local drug users, but to talk to people who could tell us about the detail of the drug market at present and about its development over time. To avoid the obvious danger that respondents might manipulate the truth in order to present themselves favourably, the drug user questionnaire contained reliability checks, with several questions repeated in slightly different ways at different points, and only information found to be reliable in this way has been used. Wherever possible, we also validated the data by checks with other sources: other interviewees or documentary evidence.

Finally, we collected supporting statistical data from the police and treatment agencies, research studies such as crime audits and community surveys, and policy documents detailing the interventions being undertaken by the various agencies.

Structure of the report

Chapter 2 of the report introduces the study neighbourhoods and describes the extent of drug market activity. The detail of the markets is described in Chapter 3, and Chapter 4 explores the impact of this activity on the neighbourhoods. In Chapter 5, we document responses to the drug markets: enforcement, treatment, prevention and education, and take a specific look at multi-agency mechanisms and how they were being used. Chapter 6 discusses these responses in the light of our knowledge of the drug market situation and the policy context. Chapter 7 sets out our recommendations.

2   Drug markets in context: eight deprived neighbourhoods

The neighbourhoods

The neighbourhoods on which this study is based were all very deprived. Most had suffered long-term economic decline. In six, the majority tenure was social housing which, by definition, caters for those on lower incomes, and has become increasingly a tenure for the most needy (Lee and Murie, 1997). Five had high proportions of private rented accommodation, a tenure that caters for people who have low capital resources (so cannot afford to buy) or who do not envisage spending a long time in one place. All of the neighbourhoods were relatively unpopular within the cities or regions in which they were located, with low housing demand and prices compared with areas around them and, as such, drew in people with little housing choice including those escaping violence, leaving prison, or moving on from hostels, and young single parents.

This combination of factors meant that the neighbourhoods exhibited high levels of disadvantage. Relative to the national average, they had very high proportions of their workforce unemployed, and higher proportions of people with weak basic skills, less likely to be able to command well-paid work. There were also relatively high proportions of non-working poor: pensioners, people who are disabled and lone parents, reflected in high levels of Income Support claims (Table 2.1). On the Index of Multiple Deprivation (DETR, 2000) Overtown and East-Docks appeared most deprived (ranking in the top 1% nationally). All the other neighbourhoods were in the top five per cent nationally except Seaview, which ranked in the top nine per cent.

Table 2.1: Indicators of deprivation for neighbourhoods

	(a) Unemployment rate December 2000 (%)	(b) % of population aged 16–60 with poor literacy skills	(c) Income support claimant rate August 1998 (%)
Range of values for study neighbourhoods	8.1 to 13.4	19.4 to 42.5	15.5 to 25.6
Mean value	9.9	32.1	18.6
England average	3.5	24.0	8.5

Notes: Data based on the electoral ward or wards most closely corresponding with the neighbourhood boundary.
a. Official ward-level unemployment data are not published. To enable a comparison, these rates are calculated using the claimant count unemployed in December 2000 (NOMIS) divided by the economically active population aged 16–59 estimated for 1998 (Oxford University population estimates for wards in England, mid 1998).
b. Source: Basic Skills Agency. Data collected in 1996/7.
c. Claimants of Income Support (DSS) divided by ward population aged 16 and over.

Areas of concentrated poverty are likely to provide fertile ground for the development of drug markets, because of higher levels of both drug use among people in disadvantaged circumstances (Parker and Bottomley, 1996; Ramsay and Partridge, 1998), and because of the likely existence of criminal networks that can readily be turned to the supply and distribution of drugs and illegal economies in which stolen goods can be exchanged (Burr, 1987). We should not be surprised to find drug market activity in these places. However, just as deprived neighbourhoods do not all exhibit similar levels of crime (Bottoms and Wiles, 1986), there is no reason to suspect that they should have similar levels, or types of drug market activity. Bottoms et al. (1989) suggest that:

"In order to understand the criminality of residential areas it is vital to consider who lives in those areas, how they come to live there in the first place, what kind of social life the residents have created and why they remain in the area and have not moved." (ibid., p.68)

Accommodation types and allocation processes, history and social and ethnic mix are all important. Since drug market transactions involve both buyers and sellers, we also suggest that location and design, determining the extent to which an area is accessed by non-residents, are also critical.

Five of the eight neighbourhoods were inner city areas, close to the facilities and transport links of the city centre. Seaview, Bankside and Riverlands were easily accessed by passers-by, while road layouts around Hilltop and East-Docks made them self-contained and less likely to be passed through by non-residents.

The inner city areas were all ethnically mixed, although in different ways. Bankside had a majority non-white population (64%), with nearly half of the population being of Pakistani origin. The other areas had much smaller ethnic communities – though still much greater than the national average of six per cent. In Riverlands and in Seaview, the largest minority group was Black Caribbean, with communities from the Caribbean being established in the area since the 1960s, and there were also smaller Asian populations. Hilltop's largest ethnic minority group was Pakistani, with smaller Black and other Asian communities. East-Docks was a predominantly white area until the 1980s, and was undergoing rapid ethnic change. The largest minority group there was Black African, from several different countries, and there were also Black Caribbean and Asian minorities. This area was the most diverse ethnically.

Table 2.2: **Ethnic composition of neighbourhoods (1991 Census)**

	% White	% Black Caribbean	% other Black	% Pakistani	% Indian/ Bangladeshi
Seaview	71	14	4	4	2
Bankside	36	1	1	49	9
Riverlands	78	10	1	1	7
Hilltop	64	3	4	20	3
East-Docks	81	5	7	1	2
Kirkside East	98	Less than 1% of any group			
Overtown	99	Less than 1% of any group			
Beachville	98	Less than 1% of any group			

The inner city areas were also diverse in their housing types and tenure (Table 2.3). Each had a mix of homes and people: large old Victorian homes converted into flats, small Victorian terraces or the tower blocks and council estates built in the 1960s, 1970s and 1980s. Although the majority of the population was stable, these areas all had above average levels of transience, mainly because they had flatted accommodation suitable for single people, who tend to move more often. All except East-Docks had over double the national average proportion of private renting. In three of the inner city areas, Riverlands,

Bankside and Seaview, our respondents identified particular pockets of transience associated with hostel provision and bed-and-breakfast accommodation. The association between homelessness and drug use is well established (e.g. Hayes and Baker, 1998; Lloyd and Griffiths, 1998). Typically, there is a high prevalence of problematic drug use among hostel dwellers. In Seaview, a hostel manager reported that 60 per cent of residents had disclosed problematic substance misuse in the last year.

Two neighbourhoods, Kirkside East and Overtown, were outer city areas, and were much less diverse in appearance and population. Their populations were almost exclusively white and culturally homogenous. Compared with the inner city areas, a higher proportion of the population had been established in the area for a long time, with a shared history and culture, and with many local family ties. Most of the homes were family houses on 1930s and 1940s estates. These areas had no hostel provision, fewer flats and lower than average private renting, and as such, had much more stable populations.

The final neighbourhood, Beachville, was a seaside town with some of the characteristics of each of the other types of neighbourhood. Part of the town had a highly transient and disadvantaged population, living in hostel or bedsit accommodation converted from hotel properties. Other parts had a much more stable population, on social housing estates or in privately owned homes. Some respondents in Beachville remarked on its distance from major centres of population, and relatively poor transport links. The population was almost exclusively white in 1991, but the recent arrival of several thousand refugees was beginning to bring ethnic and cultural change.

Table 2.3: *Housing type and tenure*

	Distance from city centre (miles)	Housing type	% Social housing	% Owner occupation	% private renting	Hostel provision?	% residents not at same address 1 year previously
Seaview	<1	Large Victorian houses converted into flats, plus 1970s low rise flats	34	50	15	Yes	17
Bankside	1.5	Large Victorian houses converted into flats. Small number of tower blocks	17	64	18	Yes?	12
Riverlands	<1	1970 and 1980s houses and flats.	54	28	16	Yes	17
Hilltop	1	Small Victorian terraces and 1970s and 1980s houses	52	34	12	No	15
East-Docks (1)	6.5	1950s and 1960s houses and flats	68	27	4	No	11
Kirkside East	4	1930s and 1940s houses. Small number of high and low rise blocks of flats	70	27	1	No	9
Overtown	5	1930s and 1940s houses. Small number of high and low rise blocks of flats	57	37	4	No	6
Beachville	N/A (not in a city)	Large former hotel properties, now hostels in and B and B. Post 1950s estates and Victorian terraces	18	65	17	Yes	14
England and Wales			68	23	7		10

Note: (1) East-Docks is in London, which has a vast city centre and inner core. While over six miles from 'the city centre' (Trafalgar Square) it had many characteristics of an inner city area. (Source: 1991 Census and fieldwork visits to neighbourhoods.)

Drug markets in the neighbourhoods

According to police, residents and drug users, all of the eight neighbourhoods had markets for illegal drugs: heroin, methadone, cocaine (powder), crack, amphetamines, ecstasy, benzodiazapines, or cannabis. In every case, the markets for heroin and crack were largely separate from the markets for drugs associated with the club scene: powder cocaine, amphetamines and ecstasy, and from the tranquilliser market. These drugs were usually supplied by different dealers, although users reported that regular dealers of one drug could often supply other drugs on request. Cannabis tended to cross into both types of market, as well as being sold by cannabis-only dealers.

We established the availability of different substances by asking users how easy it was for them to buy these drugs locally. With the exception of methadone, which varied in availability, and crack, which was not available in two of the neighbourhoods, all of the drugs we asked about were easily available in all the neighbourhoods. This report focuses on markets for crack and heroin. Heroin was easily available to users in all neighbourhoods and crack in six out of eight. Regular heroin or crack users who are familiar with supply networks in their local area will obviously find it easier to obtain these drugs than outsiders. Chapter 3 discusses drug availability and distribution networks in more detail, including the extent to which markets were open to new buyers without an introduction. In general terms, though, users in all the neighbourhoods believed that it was easy for new buyers to find suppliers with the products they wanted, either by finding someone who would introduce them to a dealer, or finding a dealer who would supply them without the need for an introduction. Some could recount their own experiences of being new in the market or starting to purchase an unfamiliar drug. Our interviewers were given the impression that it would have been easy for them to purchase drugs and, in some markets, were approached for this purpose. We feel confident in saying that in these deprived neighbourhoods illegal drugs were easily available to those who wanted to buy them.

In this chapter, we provide descriptions of the markets. We focus on the types of drugs available and prices, supply routes and distribution mechanisms and recent developments within the market, and identify different types of market associated with different types of area. The information presented here comes primarily from the interviews conducted with drug users. The police and local drug services also provided additional information.

Market histories and reputations

The majority of the markets had been established for a number of years and all but one were described as 'vibrant' and busy. Only in Beachville was the drug market more recently established and the availability of drugs limited, with a small drug-using population.

Four inner city markets (Seaview, Bankside, Riverlands and Hilltop) had long-established reputations as major drug selling places. Heroin had been widely available here since the mid-1980s and crack since the late 1980s or early 1990s. These four markets were believed to draw in drug buyers and sellers from elsewhere.

The other four markets were more localised, serving buyers from the immediate area. With the exception of Overtown, where heroin had been established since the early 1980s, these were all more recently established as heroin markets (since the early 1990s). Crack was widely available in two of these, Overtown and East-Docks, but not in the others at the time of the research. The more self-contained nature of these markets enabled firmer relationships to develop between sellers and dealers.

Price and availability

Table 3.1 shows the price and an assessment of availability for four main drugs. The prices for these drugs seemed similar across all sites, although it is likely that there is a greater variation in quantities than appears in the table, and also in quality. Prices are based on notional weights. Prices also tend to fluctuate depending on whether one was an established buyer and the quantities of drugs purchased (the more you buy the cheaper drugs are). The prices and availability rating in the table are based on our interviews with established heroin and crack users and their experiences of buying.

Price

The cost of drugs appeared to be quite consistent across the markets we visited. Heroin prices ranged between £5 and £12 for 0.1 grams (the amount of heroin usually consumed in one using event by a dependent user), the most common price being £10. A rock of crack cost between £10 and £20, and the cost of cocaine powder per gram was between £40 and £50. Methadone (linctus) was reported to cost £10 per 100 millilitres across all sites. Variations in price did not appear to be related to variations in availability[3].

In every area the price of heroin was reported to have fallen considerably in recent years. However, this reduced price was generally only available when buying larger quantities (at least a gram). Most users we spoke to still purchased heroin in smaller amounts (usually a tenth of a gram bag). The price of bags has remained stable at £10 for a number of years. This stability of prices over recent years means that the real-term cost of drugs has decreased.

Certainly, there were no price rises reported to us. In several of the markets recent developments in selling practices included the sale of heroin and crack together sometimes at a discounted rate. For example in Bankside these 'pick 'n' mix' bags consisted of a bag of heroin and a rock of crack and cost £30 which was reduced from £35. In East-Docks, if buyers made multiple purchases, discounts could be gained. It was reported that buying two rocks of crack or bags of heroin could result in a £5 discount. In areas where discounted and reduced prices were reported most of those interviewed believed that this was a result of increased availability of drugs within the market. In Kirkside East, a further market innovation was the sale of an increased range of weights. 'Bags' were sold ranging in price from £2.50 to £20.

Availability

In the majority (6) of the markets, users reported that crack and heroin were very easy to obtain. Within Bankside, Seaview and Hilltop it was reported that there were unlimited supplies of heroin and crack. Often the phrase 'awash' was used to describe the level of availability within these markets. Supplies of heroin and crack appear to have increased in recent years. In particular, crack availability has increased significantly. In one neighbourhood (Seaview) crack was reported to have overtaken heroin as the main drug in the market and in the others it had 'caught up' over the last two to three years.

---

3   The price/availability relationship in drug markets is generally not as strong as economic theory might lead one to expect. For a fuller discussion, see May et al., 2000.

Only in Kirkside East and Beachville were these drugs not as readily available. Beachville had experienced periodic heroin droughts and crack was not available. This was the only area where it was reported that policing activity had had an impact on the availability of drugs. However, even here, users maintained they only had to travel short distances in order to purchase their drug of choice. In Kirkside East, where heroin could be bought but not crack, crack users travelled to a well-established market nearby to buy the drug, and users in Beachville travelled to nearby towns, or sometimes 'washed-up' cocaine powder to make their own crack.

Table 3.1:   Cost and availability to an established buyer

Market	Heroin (per tenth of a gram)		Methadone (100 ml)		Cocaine (per gram)		Crack (per rock)	
	£	Avail.	£	Avail.	£	Avail.	£	Avail.
Seaview	10	1	10	4	50	2	10/20	1
Bankside	10	1	10	1	50	4	10/20	1
Riverlands	5	1	10	2	50	2	10	1
Hilltop	10	1	10	4	50	4	10/20	1
East-Docks	5	1	10	3	40	1	20	1
Kirkside East	10	1	10	4	50	2	20	5
Overtown	12	1	10	1	40	1	10	1
Beachville	12	1–2	10	3	45	2	20	3–4

Note: Avail. = availability rating: 1 = 'very easy' through to 5 = 'very hard'.

Drug supply and distribution

Within our eight sites, drugs entered the markets and were distributed in many different ways. Here we describe the variety of routes and mechanisms used. Table 3.2, at the end of this chapter, shows the markets at a glance.

Supply to the market

Information about drug supply was provided by users and police. The markets were supplied from both national and international sources. In Bankside, supplies of heroin came directly from outside the UK. Other areas had a number of heroin supply routes including international and national sources (Kirkside East and Overtown). There were no reports of cocaine or crack supplies coming directly from abroad even though some markets were believed to be the principal sources of crack (Bankside and Seaview) in that locality. Beachville's supplies tended to come from one or two nearby cities.

In several neighbourhoods we found supplies to the market were controlled by a handful of individuals (Hilltop and Riverlands). However, for most markets we were unable to ascertain detailed information on this.

Drug sellers

Drug selling structures varied. As mentioned above, some markets were served by a handful of suppliers. Selling drugs within these markets operated on the lines of a classic pyramid structure with a handful of suppliers supplying drugs to middle-level sellers, who (in some cases) worked with a number of small-scale sellers and runners. This was the case in Hilltop, Riverlands, Kirkside East, and Beachville and is illustrated in the case study below. The number of individuals involved in drug supply and selling varied depending on the size of the market.

In Riverlands, it was reported that the high-level sellers operated as a cartel. Around half a dozen high-level dealers supplied a core of about 20 to 30 middle-level dealers. This group supplied an estimated 60 to 70 'occasional' dealers and between 30 to 150 runners. It was reported that some small-scale dealers did operate as 'freelancers' but as they were not part of this structure, it was becoming harder for them. These small-scale sellers lack the competitive edge of the large-scale operators. In addition, disputes over competition were increasingly being resolved through violence.

In recent years, some markets had seen the proliferation of small-scale sellers as the following quote indicates:

"Everywhere you go and look you can find a dealer. In the last five years dealing has exploded." (Drug user – Bankside)

In some areas the distribution and sale of different drugs was controlled by different ethnic groups as shown in the case study below. Dorn et al. (1992) also noted separation between different ethnic groups in the market, skin colour being seen as "a useful way of delineating spheres of influence" (ibid., p.46), and giving rise to a certain amount of market stability. Our research shows that some of these established divisions were being eroded either by the introduction of new sellers (sometimes from abroad) or through greater supplies leading to sellers having greater access to a range of different drugs. In particular, the introduction of or diversification into selling crack was the main reason leading to a change in established selling patterns (Bankside, Seaview and East-Docks). These changes were also associated with increased levels of violence and firearms within some markets.

Bankside had three selling markets, although the distinction between two of the markets was becoming blurred. Both the police and drug users reported that traditionally African-Caribbean street dealers from a nearby city controlled the distribution of crack-cocaine, whilst the heroin market was dominated by Asian sellers who had grown up in the area.

The crack market was an open and relatively static street market. It was located on a central road that bisects a residential area. The epicentre of the market was positioned outside a well-known café and bookmakers shop. The police indicated that the street selling scene was highly organised and 'business-like'. Evidence from drug buyers suggested that the street crack sellers were beginning to take a greater interest in the dual sale of heroin and crack.

In contrast, the heroin market operated a closed selling structure that was highly mobile. All drug sales were arranged via cellular phones. As a rule, sales were not conducted from private residences, but 'runners' were sent to pre-arranged locations where money and drugs were exchanged. The police indicated that, unlike the crack sellers, heroin runners often tended to be users themselves. Again, evidence from drug buyers suggested that a significant number of heroin sellers were also beginning to diversify by selling crack.

Respondents indicated that the slowly eroding distinction between the two markets was causing a number of problems. Diversification by sellers from both markets was resulting in tension and friction between the two selling networks. Although, as one police officer pointed out:

"[there is a] power struggle between two very different groups – Asian males and African-Caribbean males – it is not just about drugs, but the structure of the area."

Police respondents believed that the friction between the two selling networks was responsible for an increase in firearm offences and territorial disputes. At the time of the fieldwork, the market in Bankside was in a period of transition that resulted in a volatile atmosphere for both drug users and the local community.

The majority of sellers were believed to live in the markets in which they operated. Hilltop was an extreme example of this. Selling in this area was described as being a 'closed shop' operated by those 'born and bred' in the neighbourhood. The only exceptions were in certain easily accessible inner city neighbourhoods. In Bankside, crack sellers were reported as living outside the market, and in Seaview, it was estimated that about half the sellers were outsiders.

How deals are done

In five of the neighbourhoods, the markets were primarily closed. In closed markets, access is limited to known and trusted participants. An unknown buyer needs someone to introduce them or vouch for them before they can make a purchase (May *et al.*, 2000).

In closed markets, most deals are arranged using mobile phones. Meeting or drop-off points are arranged where drugs and cash are exchanged. Buyers and sellers are wary of executing deals where they live, so most deals are completed in public places. Generally runners (individuals who deliver drugs to drug users for sellers) are sent to pre-arranged locations. Drop-off points are often alleyways, subways, bus stops, stairwells and other street-based locations. In Riverlands, the use of regular drop-off points had led to some non pre-arranged buying and selling at these points.

The remaining three neighbourhoods also had closed supply systems, but open markets existed within these areas as well. Open markets are ones where there are no barriers to access; someone completely unknown to sellers would be able to buy drugs in an open market (May *et al.*, 2000). In Bankside, crack was sold in an open street-based market, its centre being a well-known café and bookmakers. In Seaview, an open heroin and crack market operated outside a café that housed a closed market. Open selling here was mainly to new or unknown buyers and clients of sex workers. It was reported that the quality, quantity and price of drugs in open markets were inferior to that available in the closed market. In Riverlands, police operations (primarily the use of test purchasing) appear to have had some effect on the open market by reducing overt street dealing to a large extent. However, it was reported that potential buyers who 'look right' were able to successfully purchase drugs on the streets. Since most of the sales to known users still take place on the streets, the opportunity exists for new or passing buyers to make contacts without introduction.

At the time of the fieldwork, these three markets appeared to be more vulnerable to change. The distribution systems (including processes, place and players) were more fluid and responsive to changes in market conditions.

Within Seaview, a third more recently established market had existed for a short time before the fieldwork, on the periphery of the main open market. This market was targeted at new or 'green' buyers who were sold fake illicit drugs.

Runners

In four of the eight neighbourhoods runners were part of the drug distribution system. In Bankside, Seaview, Hilltop and Riverlands, they were an integral part of the market and it was clear that a large number of people were involved in this activity in these markets. Only a handful of runners was believed to operate in East-Docks and Beachville. This system may be less developed in these areas because of the smaller-scale market. Runners were generally from the neighbourhood and were young. It was clear in some areas that local youths were involved in the drug market as runners. In Seaview, drug agency staff, criminal justice agency workers and a religious leader suggested that children as young as 12 years old were fulfilling this function. In some areas, runners were also drug users. In Bankside, those running heroin were perceived as being heroin users whereas crack runners were identified as non-users.

Violence and firearms

In most of the neighbourhoods, violence and the use of firearms was becoming an increasing concern. While we cannot say with any degree of certainty whether all the incidents reported to us were a direct consequence of the drug market, many of those involved were sellers, runners or users. Several respondents reported that increased levels of violence were a function of the increase in crack trade.

Violence was used in three ways, to enforce payment of drug debts, to resolve competition between dealers, and to sanction informants.

The threat or use of violence to enforce drug debt payment was common practice in all markets. There was, however, a wide variation in levels of dealer tolerance of bad debts. The highest levels of violence were in large inner city markets, with transient populations, fluid buyer-seller relationships and a lot of competition. In Riverlands, six of the nine drug users interviewed reported being attacked, threatened or abused by dealers; one recounted how:

"A dealer threatened to kidnap and shoot me over a £80 debt." (Drug user – Riverlands)

By contrast, in areas with more stable populations and established buyer/seller relationships, extreme violence of this kind was rare. A user in Beachville, who had previously lived in inner London, described extreme violence, often over small debts, in the large inner city markets she used there, compared with her experience in the local market in Beachville where, although violence was threatened, it was not used to the same extent:

"You get it (violence) but they're plastic gangsters down here (Beachville) – all talk down here. You need to owe them big money down here before anything will happen." (Drug user – Beachville)

Only one of the drug users from any of the non-inner city areas reported experiencing violence (a black eye for non-payment of a debt). In these areas, users were more likely to be able to identify things that they liked about the area, usually the people and the community. One user indicated how these links helped to regulate the drug market.

"I know everyone. I know what's what and who to trust, how far to push. You don't get people pushing gear on kids (11-12 year olds) here. If anything bad happened here everybody would get together to sort it out." (Drug user – Kirkside East)

The second type of violence was violence to resolve competition between dealers. There were reports of firearms being used through competition between dealers in five of the drug markets. The worst levels were in the large inner city markets with high levels of competition – Riverlands, Seaview and Bankside – which attracted competition from new sellers who were not local people but outsiders, from other parts of the city or other cities. Residents and police officers gave accounts of numerous firearms incidents in each of these. As shown in the earlier case study in Bankside, diversification by sellers into the sale of crack and heroin (the police believed) had resulted in an increase of firearms offences[4]. Similarly, stable dealing relationships in East-Docks were disrupted by the arrival of a group of new sellers. Conflict arose, resulting in a firearms incident.

Thirdly, there was a widespread perception that violence was used, or would be used, to sanction informants. It was difficult to establish the extent of this activity, although there were certainly some incidents, which ranged from threats and abuse to physical attacks. Stories of such attacks are likely to have a prominent place in local folklore. Even a small number of incidents may induce a perception that informing the police about drug dealing is a dangerous business.

---

4 Reports of numerous firearm incidents were not borne out by police statistics. According to police respondents, this is because it is very rare for the public to report firearm incidents. They often only come to light if someone is hospitalised.

Involvement of young people

For four of our neighbourhoods, we are able to provide an assessment of the involvement of young people in the drug market as sellers, runners or users.

In Bankside and Seaview, young people's involvement in the market was highly visible. In Seaview, the local Youth Offending Team had seen an increase in the number of young people using both heroin and cocaine. The increase in school exclusions and a lack of recreational facilities was reported to have resulted in some young people 'hanging about' and coming into direct contact with street dealers. Dealing and running was seen as attractive because of the money that can be made, as the following quote illustrates:

> "You know how it is – 'I'm dealing this, I'm making this, I'll take care of you. I'll get you a bike and a mobile [phone], and you're away, they [the police] can't catch you. They [young dealers] are out there on the street. You can watch them with their bikes and mobiles waiting for the next call."

A drug service located in Seaview has a youth team and during 1999/2000 they worked with 400 young people and 35 parents. Although not all of these young clients were from Seaview, it highlights the growing number of young people who have problems related to drugs in this area.

Interviewees mentioned a range of factors that may influence young people to become involved in the drug market. Reasons included exclusion from school, limited recreational and economic opportunities, consumerism, and peer pressure.

By contrast, in Kirkside East we spoke with several young (under 21) heroin users who maintained that heroin use amongst their peers was not very common. Negative views and the poor image of heroin users were believed to be two of the factors influencing young people's drug choices.

Table 3.2:   The markets at a glance

	Seaview	Bankside	Riverlands	Hilltop	EastDocks	Kirkside East	Overtown	Beachville
Structure of market	Changing	Changing	Changing	Stable	Stable – some signs of recent change	Stable	Stable	Stable
Type of market	H/CR	H/CR	H/CR	H/ CR	H/CR	Heroin	H/CR	Heroin
Type of distribution	Open and Closed	Closed (H) Open (CR)	Open and Closed	Closed	Closed	Closed	Closed	Closed
Buyer/seller contact	Phone/Houses Street	Phone (H) Street (CR)	Phone/ Street	Phone	Phone	Phone	Phone/ Houses	Phone
Outside buyers	Yes	Yes	Yes	Yes	No	No	No	No
Young people involved in market (sellers, runners or buyers)	Yes	Yes	Yes	Yes	No evidence	No	No evidence	No evidence
Violence in the market	Yes	Yes	Yes	Yes	Yes	No	No	No
Use of firearms	Yes	Yes	Yes	Yes	Yes	No	No	No
New sellers	Yes	No	No	No	Yes	No	No	No

Note: H = heroin; CR = crack cocaine.

Types of drug market and the link to neighbourhood characteristics

In terms of the types of drugs available and market history, we can distinguish two main types of market found in the deprived neighbourhoods in this study (see Table 3.3).

Table 3.3:   Typology of the markets

	TYPE A : Central Place Markets	TYPE B: Local Markets
Market Characteristics	• Long-established with wide reputation as major drug market	• Established but one market among many. No specific reputation
	• Buyers from outside area as well as local	• Buyers mainly local
	• Vulnerable to competition	• Firmly established buyer/seller relationships. Less vulnerable to competition
	• Some openness and street selling	• Closed market
	• Ethnic minority group or groups mainly involved at street level	• Members of white majority group mainly involved at street level
Characteristics of Area	• Inner city	
	• Geographically 'open' area – easily passed through	• Outer city
	• Long-established ethnic minority groups with strong cultural identity	• Almost exclusively white – cultural homogeneity. Not changing in ethnic mix
	• Mixed housing types and tenure.	• Main housing type/tenure is family housing on post war council estates
	• Significant transient population associated with flats or hostels	• Little significant transient population. Very stable.
Markets in this category	• Riverlands	• Kirkside East
	• Seaview	• Overtown
	• Bankside	

Central place markets were long-established with wide reputations. As such, they drew buyers from outside the area as well as within it. There was some degree of 'open-ness' to casual buyers, and some street dealing, as well as 'closed' trade arranged by telephone through established contacts. The size, reputation and accessibility of these markets made them vulnerable to competition from new sellers trying to get a share of the sizeable trade, and market arrangements appeared to be more fluid. Conflicts between competing dealers could result in extreme violence. We found three of these markets: in Seaview, Riverlands and Bankside, all inner cities that were easy to access. Their locations helped to establish and maintain them as markets that served a wider catchment area than the neighbourhood itself. These areas all had mixed housing types and tenure (see Table 2.3), including hostel provision and flats. The availability of single person's accommodation or hostel spaces drew vulnerable people into the area, some of whom would be potential buyers. Anecdotally, it was even suggested that the combination of a central location, available accommodation and readily available drugs drew drug users in out of choice. All of these three areas also had long-standing ethnic minority populations with established social networks and a strong cultural identity. Members of these minority populations were chiefly involved in the drug market at lower levels.

Local markets were also well established, although they did not have singular reputations. Most buyers were local, with firmly established buyer/seller relationships. Local markets were less vulnerable to competition, and market arrangements were more stable. These markets were in the two outer city areas – Kirkside East and Overtown – in areas dominated by family housing and council tenure. They were very stable areas, with low transience, although they were unpopular housing areas that offered the opportunity for vulnerable people to move in. Both areas had significant numbers of empty properties. The communities in these areas were almost exclusively white. Family ties, social networks and norms had been established over several generations. These were areas where many people knew each other and there was great homogeneity of culture. Virtually all of the people involved in the drug markets at street level were members of the white community and many were connected with established criminal networks and the illegal economy as well as the drug trade. These markets resemble that described by Parker *et al.* (1998) in another white working class community. Users and residents reported vigilante action against drug users and dealers in these markets.

Of the remaining markets, the two in the other inner city areas had characteristics of both Central Place and Local. Both of these were in areas slightly less accessible and more self-contained than the Central Place markets, but more accessible, transient and culturally diverse than the local markets. Hilltop was a well-known market, one of two main markets in the city and did attract outside buyers, although there were also firmly established buyer/seller relationships, and no open dealing. It was vulnerable to competition, but was firmly controlled by established sellers who had successfully beaten off rivals. Most higher-level sellers were from the established majority white community in the area, not the ethnic minority groups. However, ethnic minority groups were involved in the lower echelons of the dealing structure. East-Docks was a lesser-known market, one of several locally, and until very recently, had not been open to competition. Buyer/seller relationships were strongly established and there was no open dealing. In contrast to Hilltop, most of those involved in the selling were from the minority ethnic communities, not from the white majority.

The final market was in Beachville, the seaside town. This was a much smaller market, and more recently established. Its location in a small town, distant from others, meant that it served a much smaller catchment area and that buyers were local. It was also more detached from supply networks and from outside competition. This was a predominantly white area and the control of the drug market reflected the population composition.

In the remaining chapters, we note how the impact of drug markets and the responses of local agencies and communities varied by market type.

4   Neighbourhood impacts

In this chapter, we examine the impact of the drug markets on their neighbourhoods. We investigated a number of issues: crime committed by drug users, violence, neighbourhood nuisance, discarded used needles in public spaces, and issues relating to the risk of young people becoming involved in drug market activity. All the information is based on our interviews with a relatively small number of local residents, drug users and professionals familiar with the areas, backed by community surveys where available. This is not unproblematic. Dorn *et al.* (1987) demonstrate that people in different positions, with different perspectives and different kinds of knowledge about drug markets, see the local impact of drug markets in distinct ways.

> "To a large extent, signs are socially constructed and what people take as an indication of concrete evidence is a negotiated process conducted in local forums where different groups have different interests." (ibid., p.39)

They suggest, nevertheless, that some identification of what is going on, and of the impact it has, is possible, if information is gathered from a variety of sources, and this was our approach. Discussion of our findings with a selection of our original respondents indicated that they reflected 'reality' as perceived from a variety of angles.

Crime committed by drug users

Previous research shows a strong link between heroin and crack cocaine use and some forms of crime (Parker *et al.*, 1998; Edmunds *et al.*, 1998 & 1999; Turnbull *et al.*, 2000). Bennett (1998) found a 'statistically significant correlation' over four measures of drug use and crime among arrestees leading him to conclude:

> "There is clear evidence that as drug use increases involvement in criminal behaviour increases. However, it cannot be assumed from this that drug use causes offending or that offending causes drug use." (1998, p.77)

Research suggests illicit earnings in excess of £20,000 by people using heroin and crack together, with a lower average of £4,000 to £6,000 by drug users not using heroin or crack (Bennett, 1998; Brain *et al.*, 1998). Bennett's study is only of arrestees, and therefore not a reflection of the whole drug using population, but our work too shows a strong association between drug use and crime, even though no causal connection can be firmly demonstrated. Fifty-four (out of 55) users in our sample had a history of committing crime, most reporting that they had committed their first crime in their early teens. Problematic users were spending considerable sums on drugs. The median expenditure on drugs was £170 per week (£8,840 per year) and the range was between £20 and £1200 per week.

The most common means of raising cash for drugs was shoplifting (retail theft), as shown in Table 4.1. In most of the areas, respondents noted that there was a thriving black market for stolen goods. In some cases, goods were traded openly in pubs or through door-to-door selling. Some users reported being engaged in 'shoplifting to order', often for relatively low-value goods such as batteries and children's clothing.

Table 4.1:   Users' responses to 'three main ways of financing drug use'

Area	No. of users	Burglary	Car crime	Retail theft	Robbery	Fraud	Sex work	Drug selling	Legal means
Bankside	7	3	0	4	1	2	2	2	5
Riverlands	9	2	2	7	1	0	1	2	3
Hilltop	7	1	0	3	2	3	1	1	5
East-Docks	9	2	2	1	3	2	1	0	7
Overtown	6	3	1	5	0	3	0	2	1
Beachville	6	2	2	4	0	0	0	2	0
TOTAL	44	13	7	24	7	10	5	9	21

Notes: (1) In Seaview and Kirkside East, the first two areas, respondents were not asked directly how they funded their drug use. This question was asked at a later date. (2) Legal means included work, borrowing, Job Seekers Allowance, selling possessions. These often took place alongside illegal means.

Burglary was a relatively uncommon means of financing drug use. In general terms, these findings echo those of Bennett (1998), who found that only a low number of arrestees (11%) using heroin and crack cocaine said they had committed a residential burglary in the last 12 months. Our findings show slightly higher frequency of burglary, although the sample is obviously far too small to draw any meaningful comparisons.

In some areas, we found strong counter-pressures against committing burglary locally to fund a drug habit. In three of the neighbourhoods, East-Docks, Kirkside East, and Overtown, all areas with stable communities and particularly long-established network ties, some residents and users reported that the fact that drug users were from the area and had many local contacts could deter them from stealing from neighbours. Users who admitted to burglary to fund their habit often did so with the qualification: but 'not on the estate', or 'not from council houses'. This sentiment reflected a wider-held norm in the communities that you 'do not steal from your own'. This was clearly not a universal rule – one respondent revealed that he had burgled a nearby house to pay for drugs. And concepts of 'community', 'local' and 'neighbours' were undefined. These factors might have very localised effects that do not appear in crime data. In all of these three areas, users reported vigilante action against people who committed local crime to pay for drugs. The levels of action were most significant in Overtown. When asked if they had ever experienced violence in the drug market, five of the six drug users reported receiving violence, threats, and/or abuse from 'vigilantes'. One gave an account (repeated by another, unconnected, user) of:

"A lad that got kidnapped and locked in a bin shed for three days – they broke every finger, his arm, toes... he didn't go to the police... He told us it was because he'd left needles around the place, but I think it was because he'd been burgling houses in the area." (Drug user – Overtown)

It is impossible to establish what proportion of local crime was committed by drug users. All of the study areas had relatively high crime compared with city and national averages. However, crime rates for the study areas show falling rates of burglary, in line with national trends. In a number of areas, this was also remarked upon by residents. For example:

"A couple of years ago, I'd get three or four customers telling me that they, or somebody they knew, had been burgled (every week). Now it's the odd one... every two or three weeks." (Café owner – Kirkside East)

House burglary is possibly a less effective way of raising cash sums than it used to be, because of the falling value of electrical goods and possibly because, with lower unemployment and increased credit availability, more people can afford goods new. One police officer commented:

"Six years ago everything went in a burglary – the TV, video, jewellery and any cash; four years ago they left the television; now they leave the video and just take jewellery and cash. They need to do eight burglaries now to make the same amount (as they did six years ago)." (Police officer – Riverlands).

Yet, the reported increase in use of drugs does not appear have resulted in higher rates of burglary in these drug market areas. Possibly, the risks associated with burglary outweigh the diminishing rewards.

Violence

As we reported in Chapter 3, levels of drug-related violence appear to be increasing, particularly the use of firearms. In areas where this was the case, extreme violence either experienced, witnessed, talked about or reported in the newspaper caused widespread fear.

The immediate impact of fear of violence is that residents are unwilling to give information to the police, for fear of reprisal. This was reported in all the more violent markets. For example, the local police inspector in Riverlands reported that intelligence had 'dried up' since the shootings. Even in less violent areas, fear of reprisal was an issue:

> "I wouldn't tell the police about drug dealers because it's too much of a risk with your house. Quite a few people have said they tell the police and they (the police) say they won't say anything but then the people's windows go through." (Parent – Kirkside East)[5]

Fear of reprisal affected residents' willingness to become involved in collective action against drugs. We found only one example of collective resident action against drugs, in Seaview, where the residents association was considering establishing a 'mothers against drugs' project, but was concerned about reprisals for people involved. In Overtown, a drug prevention worker gave the example of a resident:

> "...who set about leafleting local residents asking 'are you fed up with drug dealers?'. She was going to distribute them but I asked her to think of the consequences." (Drug prevention worker – Overtown)

The worker added that she had advised the woman not to put her home telephone number on the leaflets.

Evidence from our areas suggests that violence does not prevent a sense of community developing, nor prevent collective action more generally. Indeed, in one area (Seaview), increasing violence had prompted members of the local community to enter into dialogue with the police. However, it may inhibit community interaction. In Riverlands, for example, a resident described how, since the increase in violence, she had become much more guarded in talking to her neighbours, and a local professional described how the power of the drug sellers (expressed through violence) and the failure of the police to protect residents and witnesses from intimidation had effectively disempowered the community. Bourgois, writing about the impact of crack in America, also referred to the potential of 'terror' to isolate people from the community and create distrust of neighbours (1995, pp.34-5).

---

5   Interview conducted by Helen Bowman as part of CASE's Neighbourhood Study.

By contrast, according to residents in Overtown, successful enforcement activity that broke a 'climate of intimidation' imposed by drug dealers resulted in a revitalisation of community activities such as youth activities, trips and an estate festival, because the confidence of residents had been restored[6].

Neighbourhood nuisance

Neighbourhood nuisance was one of the main problems associated with certain prominent drug markets in our earlier work (Lupton, 2001). These concerns related to disturbance associated with a large number of visits to certain properties or public places. However, these problems were rarely raised by residents in this research. Dorn et al.'s work (1987) showed that the structure of dealing was an important factor determining its local visibility and impact. It seems likely that changes in the structure of dealing (with deals more likely to be made by mobile phone) have contributed to reducing these impacts. Users waiting for a deal to be dropped off usually hang around alone or in twos, still in public places (such as at a bus shelter, outside a shop, pub or phone box) but not necessarily fixed sites. However, a comment from a resident in East-Docks about "teenagers... waiting for a delivery on street corners and outside phone boxes" shows that the changed dealing method has not made the trade entirely invisible.

Discarded used needles

According to our respondents, discarded used needles were not regarded as a problem in four of the neighbourhoods – Seaview, Hilltop, Beachville and Overtown. In the others, they presented a localised problem in specific drug-using sites, causing concern for residents, especially those with children. For example a professional working close to one of main sites for discarded needles in Riverlands spoke of the way that:

> "Heroin use has placed the playing field out of bounds for the community and the school. During a recent attempt to clean it up, they found more than 50 needles in one hour. There are needles all around the nearby flats – people using the stairwells to shoot up in." (Regeneration manager – Riverlands)

When asked what they did not like about the area two of the drug users from this area cited used needles "in the streets and everywhere". This was also reported as a problem in Bankside in and around the limited number of council-owned flats. The Neighbourhood Housing Manager stating that discarded syringes and foil were a problem for residents in specific locations and one non-statutory housing provider commented:

---

6   See Chapter 5 for a fuller description of this initiative.

"There is a set of low-rise flats. I've had tenants in saying that they find needles regularly in their stairways." (Neighbourhood advice service provider – Bankside)

In two areas, Kirkside East and Overtown, respondents noted that the problem of discarded needles seemed to have lessened in recent years. For example, in East-Docks, a street cleaner reported frequent finds behind the shops in the main shopping area, but a local vicar noted a reduction in the problem within the residential area.

"When we first moved to the area (five years previously) we used to find syringes every day in our garden, loads of them. They were also found in the park. Now you don't come across them – only very occasionally in the park. But it isn't an issue now." (Reverend – East Docks)

It was impossible to establish the reasons for this change.

Issues relating to young people becoming involved in the drug market

In most areas (particularly the Central Place markets), concerns were expressed about the possible involvement of young people in the drug market, not just as users (a widespread concern generally in society) but in selling. Sellers appeared to have a high profile, success, and high social status that could be a draw for young people, especially in the absence of other opportunities. These views, which have also been observed in other studies (Dorn et al., 1992) were expressed by young people, older residents and professionals. For example:

"The younger generation are being influenced by the fact that dealers are getting away with it [dealing] and getting the high life. They see the dealers chilling out in their fancy cars with their gold chains and their girlfriends, and they've got cash coming out of their ears. Young people then aspire... they look at them as role models, and that's quite a disturbing fact." (Young person – Bankside)

"It is now a good thing to deal, not a bad thing." (Respondent – Bankside)

"There is a lot of it about, it is becoming a normal thing, it does not shock anyone anymore." (Respondent – Bankside)

Respondents commented that drug selling and buying had a high visibility, and had, to a certain extent. become normalised, creating extra pressures to become involved.

Unsurprisingly, we found that parents were particularly sensitised to these concerns, although levels of concern did vary depending on where people lived (in relation to the main drug market), and according to their confidence in other influences on their children.

> "I don't worry about it [drugs]. Mine [my children] were brought up to know better. I know where they are and they tell me what they're doing." (Parent – Overtown)

Levels of knowledge about drugs also seemed to have an impact on levels of concern. A number of older residents we spoke to were very concerned about the risks of drugs to young people but were unable to distinguish between risks, for example between cannabis and heroin. Dorn *et al.* (1987) also reported this finding. In both Hilltop and Overtown, drug awareness and prevention projects were working with parents as well as with young people.

The overall impact of the drug markets

Overall, drug markets ranked among the highest concerns of residents in these neighbourhoods, but were not necessarily their greatest concern. Community surveys showed that in East-Docks, crime and anti-social behaviour by young people ranked more highly among residents' priorities for action. In Kirkside East, it ranked below burglary and youth crime, and similar results were found in Hilltop, Riverlands and Overtown. The precise impact of the market could always be contested. In Overtown, for example, suggestions by the housing manager that drug selling was causing housing abandonment were contradicted by residents of the street, who cited youth crime and disturbance as the main factor. And similar levels of activity appeared to impact differently in different places, according to the physical layout of the area, variations in the using population, methods of buying and selling, and the extent to which dealers and users were local people, as well as according to who defined the problem, and their other priorities and responsibilities.

In general, however, we found that the drug market seemed to be one issue having a negative impact on neighbourhood quality of life and young people's prospects, but not the only one. It was not, on its own, a sufficient condition for neighbourhood decline, but a contributory factor. We found no evidence that drug markets alone were driving people away from areas in significant numbers, although this dynamic did appear to be at work in one of the pilot study sites. In no area did a vibrant and disruptive drug market occur without the presence of other neighbourhood problems, such as anti-social behaviour, high crime, poor quality housing, lack of local employment, or a bad reputation. The impact of all such factors is heightened in situations of housing oversupply, where people have a choice to move.

However, markets could also constrain regeneration prospects by reputation. Most of the areas suffered from reputations as places where drugs could be bought and sold. The market was not the only aspect of their negative labelling by the media and in local folklore – most also had long-standing reputations as being rougher or more dangerous than other places – but it contributed an additional stigma. For example, when asked how drug dealing had affected the decline of the area, a professional, resident in Riverlands for 23 years, replied that:

> "It has a reputation for drugs and shootings. This has added to an already bad reputation." (Resident – Riverlands)

Respondents commented that such reputations, whether justified or not, had an impact on residents' confidence, chances of gaining credit (and thus incurring debt by being forced to borrow money at higher rates) and on housing demand. In Hilltop, a housing worker commented that,

> "I think that for families then the issues of drugs and crime is very important and people want to move their families from that." (Housing worker – Hilltop)

And in Kirkside East, the housing manager recalled how already low housing demand "flattened overnight" after a national television documentary that labelled it "the needle capital of the north", in the mid-1990s. Demand is still among the lowest in the city, and the reputation has stuck.

> "I wouldn't say that the area is notably worse than the ones surrounding – they have similar problems, but Kirkside East just has the reputation for drugs in the same way that [another area] has a reputation for joyriding – high profile, but no worse than the other areas." (Police officer – Kirkside East)

It is difficult to see how community confidence could be restored without tackling both the drug market problem and the attendant labelling.

5   Local responses

Drug markets can be tackled at local level by reducing both supply and demand (Newburn and Elliott, 1998; Jacobson, 1999). The need for both has been recognised in the drugs policy of successive governments. Local supply reduction involves arresting suppliers or making their activity so risky that they stop it or take their trade elsewhere. Demand reduction can occur through education and prevention strategies – to try to prevent drug use, limit it or delay its onset – or through treatment of existing users. Since problematic drug users with frequent use account for a large proportion of market transactions, local treatment interventions can have a significant impact on market activity.

In this chapter, we document the interventions in the neighbourhoods we studied and look at the extent to which interventions of different agencies were co-ordinated. It was not our remit to evaluate these initiatives. Hence, we have only been able to make comments on their quality and effectiveness where these were specifically made available to us through prior evaluations or the assessment of key actors. Our aim is to document the overall extent of the response, in relation to the problems we described in Chapters 3 and 4.

Supply reduction through enforcement strategies

Enforcement activity in most markets was limited to policing, including both major operations and routine low-level activity.

In the period before our fieldwork, only three areas had implemented major policing operations. Riverlands had the most significant and sustained activity. A major city-wide operation had been running for about 18 months, in response to shootings arising from conflicts between rival dealers. Initially, a dedicated team of ten officers targeted street-level dealers, disrupting the market and causing instability, so that a longer-term strategy of trying to infiltrate dealing networks above street level could be implemented. In the first phase, a number of successful arrests were made using test purchases, and convictions have followed. At the time of the fieldwork, the squad was in the second phase of the operation. Local officers acknowledged its marked short-term impact, but doubted that it would stem the growth of the market overall.

In Overtown, we were told about a very successful policing operation several years ago on one particular estate. As well as policing, the operation involved the use of situational measures, restricting access to the estate, and also demonstrated the importance of working with active residents and capitalising on their determination to deal with the problem. However, while successful in the short-term, this operation did not stem the overall development of the market in the area. During our fieldwork, users reported that both heroin and crack were more widely available than they were in the mid-1990s, though not from these specific sites.

One estate in Overtown reached a serious situation in 1994, when nuisance and traffic associated with drug dealing and intimidation by dealers drove law-abiding residents away and made the estate a no-go area for the police, and for contractors who were starting to undertake Estate Action improvements. Problems were concentrated in one crescent where 24 out of 100 homes were empty, many of them seriously vandalised. Dealers allowed rotting rubbish to accumulate in the front gardens and stored drugs in it, to avoid detection. There was serious intimidation. In the words of a senior police officer "the balance of power had shifted to the criminals", and one user we interviewed, who had been dealing on the crescent in this period, confirmed that "the situation had got right out of hand ... it was mental". She confirmed that buyers came from towns up to 50 miles away.

Apart from the intimidation, the estate was difficult to police, with five vehicle entry points, leading onto two major dual carriageways out of the town. Buyers were gone before police could attend the scene. Changing the access was a pre-requisite of an effective policing operation. In 1995, one of the main entry points to the estate was closed off to prevent through traffic, and police undertook high visibility policing, moving vans onto the estate and parking them outside the main dealer's house. Visitors to the close were stopped and searched, with 43 arrests made in two weeks. Bolstered by this activity, residents formed an action committee and began to work closely with police and housing, liaising over police action and estate improvements. The troublesome crescent was divided into two cul-de-sacs. This action stopped through traffic, involved the demolition of some of the empty properties, and isolated the remaining dealers in a short cul-de-sac. The problem completely stopped. Estate improvements were undertaken, which made the estate more popular and generated a small waiting list. The police were able to restore a community officer to the estate, and the residents association began to restore normal community activities, and, encouraged by its success, to consider establishing a tenant management organisation.

Routine policing strategies involved low-level enforcement tactics, with the objective not of eradicating the drug market, but rather 'managing' it, trying to keep it from growing or causing too much disruption locally. This objective was explicitly acknowledged by police officers in a number of areas. For example:

"We manage the drugs problem. We will never clear this country of drugs, ever. What we do, the police, is we manage what we've got. We tend to react to it so that we can keep a lid on it and it doesn't get any worse than it already is because it is pretty damn bad now. And we do, we just manage it." (Police Inspector – Hilltop)

The fact that low-level enforcement has a limited effect does not mean it is not worth doing. Edmunds et al. (1996) suggested that there are gains from low-level enforcement. 'Collateral damage' suffered by communities may be limited, the reputation of the market may suffer, and, while there may be some displacement, this is unlikely to be total. Clearly, the impact of enforcement action will depend on its intensity and frequency and the appropriateness of its targeting. Low-level tactics in the markets in this study included stop-and-search, test purchase operations and intelligence-led policing (including the use of registered sources).[7]

Stop-and-search was used in all the markets. Test purchase had a more limited use, mainly because a large proportion of the markets now operated a closed selling system, and was becoming a less useful tool. Sellers were increasingly demanding that new buyers should smoke purchased drugs in their presence, making this too risky a strategy for officers to pursue. In all markets, police respondents also cited the use of informants and intelligence-led policing as one of their main enforcement strategies (see also Newburn and Elliott, 1998; Chatterton et al., 1998). In most cases (except Beachville, which we discuss later) it was unclear as to what officers were incorporating within the terms 'intelligence' and 'informant'. 'Intelligence' could refer to information gathered from unofficial informants, anonymous or public sources (all referred to under the general term 'informants') as well as registered police sources.

The police regarded enforcement actions as being effective only in the short-term. Officers in all areas except Beachville were unanimous in their agreement that current enforcement strategies had no long-term effect on drug selling in their respective markets. In contrast to Edmunds et al.'s study of six markets in London in 1996, where "respondents were preoccupied about enforcement activities" (p.vi) users in all markets in this study except one (Beachville) reported very little disruption of their activities by police, and concurred with the police view that enforcement activity tended to have little long-term impact. This example is typical:

---

7   Given the sensitivity of the subject matter, it is likely that there was wider use of enforcement techniques than actually reported to us.

"[the raid] had no effect at all. Within half an hour, all the dealers were back. They were wary for a couple of hours, but then it was back to normal." (Drug buyer – Bankside)

Routine enforcement activity was, in some cases, supplemented by specific initiatives to work with the community and other agencies against the drug market. In Bankside, the police deployed 'Community Intervention Officers' who worked with the community, schools and the youth service with a brief to tackle drugs in the community, instigate community safety schemes and divert young people from crime and drugs. In Seaview, a hostel worker described good working arrangements with local police, whereby the hostel had a named police officer to contact if drug dealing or violence occurred on or near the hostel premises. The officer had an ongoing relationship with the hostel and could initiate an appropriate police response. Despite these kinds of initiatives, in most areas there was substantial resident dissatisfaction with the level of police activity to combat the drug market, and with its impact. For example :

"There is a feeling in this community that the police know there is drug dealing going on all around but they just don't do anything…" (Agency professional – Seaview)

Beachville was the only area where respondents concurred that low-level enforcement was effective to any degree. Policing of the drug market in this area involved intelligence-led policing and high visibility policing of hotspots. The police force in this area made a heavy investment in intelligence capacity, and there was a clear strategy in relation to drugs intelligence. Intelligence gathered from all sources was used to map all levels of the drug market, from supply networks to outlets for stolen goods. From this information strategic targets were generated, enabling officers to target all dealing levels within the market. One part of Beachville was a crime and drug hotspot that the police had made a commitment to tackle. Intelligence gathering was coupled with other methods, including the installation of CCTV and the specific deployment of officers from an enforcement unit of uniformed constables. These officers were deployed in the area on a long-term basis, giving it more officers per square mile then anywhere else in the force area. Their activities included stop-and-search and warrant execution. As a result, the market in Beachville was regularly disrupted. Drug users in Beachville reported frequent 'hassle' by police, even leading them to carry drugs internally to avoid detection. There was certainly inconvenience to users, which may have limited market growth. However, it was not clear to what extent these tactics led to reduced availability of drugs. Occasional heroin droughts were reported in the area, but this may also have been due to limited supply routes.

Civil sanctions, such as the use of anti-social behaviour orders (ASBOs) and enforcement of tenancy conditions, could also, in theory, be used against drug sellers. One police respondent explained the potential of these measures:

> "We are working with housing to serve ASBOs on dealers, destabilise them. They like a stable workbase. We're going to keep hitting their address – keep them on the move." (Divisional Police Commander – Kirkside East)

However, in practice, no ASBOs had been issued against drug sellers in this area or others. Only two ASBOs had been issued at all, for any offence. Possession orders could also be used in social housing areas where drug-selling activities caused a breach of tenancy conditions. In three areas police and housing departments were working closely together (in one case through a 'Combined Response Team') to gather evidence against problematic tenants, and to work proactively with potentially difficult tenants moving from other areas. However, as with ASBOs, there were, in practice, very few drug-related cases; most related to noise and nuisance.

Demand reduction: drug services

Services for drug users were of three main kinds: generic treatment agencies offering a range of interventions including needle exchange, counselling and complementary therapies, methadone prescription for opiate users, and specialist services for particular groups of users. There was a consensus among the treatment providers we interviewed that problem users rarely have the funds to travel any great distance (probably not more than about two miles), and are often unaware of generic services outside their immediate locality. For specialist services, they may travel further. We looked, therefore, at generic treatment service close to the markets, and at specialist services slightly further afield. Table 5.1 summarises the extent of treatment provision. We found considerable variation between areas, particularly between inner city areas, which had a wider range of services, and others.

All of the areas except two had generic drug treatment services provided by statutory or non-statutory services, or both. These could be directly accessed and typically offered a wide range of interventions, including needle exchange, acupuncture, hepatitis B and C screening, hepatitis B immunisation, and a selection of other services including herbal remedies or relapse prevention. They saw large numbers of clients. Kirkside East and Beachville had no local treatment agencies, the nearest being four and eight miles away respectively, although outreach was provided in Beachville at the local youth project and at its alcohol centre in the town and in Kirkside East, the shared care worker provided a range of services upon referral by the GP.

In Seaview, the non-statutory service provided a drop-in, a needle exchange facility, specialist services for female drug users, a brief interventions programme, complementary therapies, shared care with local general practitioners, housing support, a relapse avoidance programme, and outreach work. There were also several criminal justice intervention projects run in conjunction with the probation service the youth offending team and the local prison CARAT workers. The service saw 3,523 individuals in a year. This number will include drug users who do not use Seaview to purchase drugs, but will also under-represent ethnic minority and stimulant drug users.

One of the strengths of the service was the variety of programmes that were run in partnership with other services. An innovative development was a 'core assessment' tool that could be used by all agencies in contact with drug users. The use of this tool aims to avoid duplication and ensure compatibility of information. The project manager believed that – if successful – it would reduce the need for individuals to be re-assessed each time they passed through a different treatment agency. Another benefit would be a reduction in waiting times.

In all areas apart from three (Hilltop, Seaview and Riverlands), users (and occasionally referring agencies) were critical of treatment provision. In some cases, these criticisms related to the failure of the services to react to local conditions. For example, in Bankside, a predominantly Asian area with both heroin and crack markets, a wide range of services was provided. However, respondents suggested that, apart from its needle exchange, the agency did not attract chaotic dual users, ethnic minority clients (only 8% of clients were from an ethnic minority), or female drug users (9:1 male/female ratio recorded in the needle exchange). Of the drug users we interviewed, all knew of the service but few had attended any of the programmes. The service appeared to attract drug users who were relatively stable or those who were determined to cease using illicit drugs.

Table 5.1: *Services available within a two-mile radius of the drug market*

Services	Inner city areas						Others	
	Seaview	Bankside	Riverlands	Hilltop	East-Docks	Kirkside East	Overtown	Beachville
Generic services								
Statutory service	Yes	No	Yes	No	No	No[1]	No	No[2]
Voluntary service	Yes	Yes	Yes	Yes	Yes	No	Yes	No
Outreach work	Yes	Yes	No	Yes	No	No	Yes	Yes
Detoxification beds (No. available in city)	DK	0	5	5	2	0	2	0
Methadone prescribing								
DDU	Yes	Yes	Yes	No[3]	Yes[4]	No	No	No
Shared care	Yes	No	Yes	Yes	No	Yes	Yes	No
Prescribing GPs	Yes	No	Yes	No	Yes	Yes	Yes	Yes
Specialist services								
Specialist stimulant service	No	No	No	No	Yes	No	No	No
Stimulant service within drug service	Yes	Yes	Yes	Yes	No	No	Yes	Yes
Youth service (for drugs)	Yes	Yes	Yes	No	Yes	No	Yes	No
Specialist ethnic minority service	Yes	No	Yes	Yes	Yes	No	No	No
Sex work service	Yes	Yes	Yes	No	No	No	No	No

Notes: (1) Outreach service provided via shared care arrangement; (2) Outreach service provided; (3) Low threshold maintenance programme for 25 users assisted by a nurse; DK = Don't know. (4) Via a satellite service at the Community Drug Team;

In other cases, the criticisms were about the capacity of services. For example, in East-Docks, the local non-statutory agency appeared to react to the needs of specialist groups but did not have a generic service that was able to cope with, or attract clients in the area[8]. Drug users commented that the staff in one agency did not have the time to provide a service they felt adequately addressed their drug use. This service accepted all referrals. In Overtown, treatment for drug users was provided by one local community drug team (CDT). Unlike the service in East-Docks, this team only took a fixed number of clients, and operated a waiting list. Users commented on difficulty getting access to the service. An extra worker was about to be appointed. Extra workers were being appointed in several of the services we looked at, with the expansion of treatment funding announced by the government in 2000. We did not, however, see any wholly new services, nor hear of any increase in residential or detoxification provision. As Table 5.1 demonstrates, detoxification beds were very limited in number.

Outreach services were provided by some but not all agencies. One treatment agency near Riverlands did not provide outreach in the area because they felt it was too dangerous, although another service was providing outreach work to sex workers. Concerns about violence were also expressed as a reason for not conducting outreach work in Kirkside East.

Methadone prescribing (alongside other treatment options) has been widely accepted as assisting many drug users in reducing their heroin consumption[9] and was provided in all eight areas. The main mechanisms were Drug Dependency Units (DDUs), where prescribing takes place at a specialist clinic, and shared care arrangements (whereby clients access methadone through their GPs, working alongside treatment agencies). Two areas also had GP surgeries prescribing methadone (without shared care arrangements). In Hilltop, the local generic treatment service offered a methadone maintenance service for 25 clients through a shared care arrangement assisted by a nurse.

By contrast, there were few services for crack users. Crack has been used in the United Kingdom since around 1983 (Haynes, 1998), and the need for effective treatment, independent of that provided to opiate users, has been identified for some time.

None of the areas in this study provided specialist crack services even though crack was prolific, and increasing, in a number of markets. Crack services were incorporated into existing services but drug users often perceived these services to be for opiate users.

---

8   Figures from the agency's previous quarterly report state that there were only seven referrals from the East-Docks area.

9   There are also counter-arguments that state that methadone substitution can be as harmful and addictive as heroin itself.

Although all of the statutory services and a number of voluntary services in the eight markets provided complementary therapies[10], these services were often poorly attended by primary crack users and retaining clients was reported to be difficult. Haynes *et al.* (2000) in their advisory document to the United Kingdom Anti-Drugs Co-ordination Unit (UKADCU) stated that often crack clients do not re-present to treatment services because drug agency workers respond to their needs in the same way as they do opiate clients[11].

The nearest approximation to a crack service was in East-Docks, where the Community Drug Team had set up a separate stimulant service, with a harm reduction approach using formal group sessions, acupuncture, meditation and relapse prevention. Crack users made up 60 to 70 per cent of its clients. This service illustrates some of the difficulties in crack treatment. It was running below capacity and the manager believed that this was not because there were too few crack users in the area, but that they were not engaging with the service. Only between 10 to 15 per cent of clients became abstinent. In only two other areas were crack services being actively considered at the time of fieldwork.

We also looked at services targeted at specific groups of users: ethnic minority users, young people and sex workers. Provision was variable. Four of the five areas with significant ethnic minority populations had specialist services for at least some of those users. In three areas where there was an active sex market there were specialist services for the workers. These were well regarded. Specific youth provision was available in five of the areas, even though in all eight professional workers expressed concern about the incidence of young people becoming involved in problematic illicit use. One of the potential benefits of shared care is the ability to provide treatment for young people in settings not dominated by adult users. In Kirkside East, for example, the shared care worker (a Community Psychiatric Nurse) worked from the local medical centre, seeing young people individually when they had consulted their GP.

Demand reduction: education

Drug education is a statutory requirement under the national curriculum. Beyond this, it may be provided in a number of ways: by schools, with specific drug education programmes as part of their personal, social and health education, by youth services, and by voluntary and community organisations.

---

10 Complementary therapies included: acupuncture, reflexology, relaxation, and in one agency (Hilltop) liver wellness.
11 Haynes *et al.* (2000) stated that crack users' needs are different from opiate clients in a number of ways. Often this is due to irrational behaviour patterns. Drug agency staff should therefore be aware of this and provide appropriate support and services, which will not necessarily be the same as services for opiate users.

DATs are required to monitor drug education and can access funding for this purpose. Four of the eight DATs could not provide this information in full[12]. The evidence from the remaining areas suggests that drug education programmes are provided in virtually all secondary schools and a majority of primary schools (Table 5.2), although these data only apply to the DAT areas as a whole, not to the study neighbourhoods in particular. These programmes are now expected to be delivered to the National Healthy Schools Standard (NHSS) or its equivalent set by the Standing Conference on Drug Abuse (now Drugscope). These standards are based on the premise that drug education should be accurate, impartial, credible and help to enable young people to make informed choices about their drug use rather than trying to shock or deter them. Table 5.2 indicates that few schools were making progress towards the adoption of these standards, with the exception of those in the DAT area containing Bankside.

Table 5.2: **Level of drug education provision in schools**

	State primary schools in DAT area with drug education (DE) programmes	State secondary schools in DAT area with DE programmes	Primary schools which will achieve NHSS* by April 2002	State secondary schools which will achieve NHSS* by April 2002
Seaview	85%	100%	6%	0%
Bankside	72%	93%	50%	50%
East-Docks	55%	100%	Not adopting	No plan to adopt
Kirkside East	53%	98%	7%	7%
Beachville	N/K	N/K	0%	0%

Note: * NHSS = National Healthy Schools Standard. The DAT in Hilltop did not respond. DATs in Riverlands and Overtown did not include this information in their annual report. Subsequent information from Overtown revealed that 100 per cent of secondary schools have a DE programme. The standard is currently being assessed. Overtown schools are committed to the NHSS.

Schools in most of the neighbourhoods we visited used outside agencies to deliver drug education. The police were the lead agency in Riverlands and Beachville. In East-Docks, the local treatment agency provided drug education to schools under a specific youth awareness programme. In Hilltop, the Single Regeneration Budget (SRB) funded a city-wide education project providing drugs education for pupils and staff in primary schools, and Kirkside East also had a mobile unit visiting primary schools and providing drug education as part of a broader

---

12 Two DATS did not include the information in their annual reports. One only included information on targets, not the current situation, and one did not respond to the research team's requests to supply an annual report.

programme. Overtown has received funding from the Standards Fund to employ a full-time school drugs worker. We were not in a position to assess the quality of any of this work.

Outside school, formal drug education is rarely delivered, although awareness sessions are sometimes provided at youth clubs or treatment agencies. All of these organisations are, of course, only in touch with relatively small numbers of young people, not all of whom are concerned about drugs (Ward and Rhodes, 2001). Youth services in five neighbourhoods provided us with information about drug education. There was no structured education provision in any of these. Youth workers respond to individual queries according to service guidelines, provide information in leaflet form and signpost to relevant agencies. The extent of drugs knowledge among youth workers will inevitably vary. In the city containing Kirkside East, a survey of youth workers showed that only 25 per cent were either very or fairly familiar with drugs guidelines and that handing out a leaflet was the most common response. In three areas, the youth service arranged drug awareness sessions given by treatment agencies and in one of these, Overtown, there was a close relationship between youth agencies and drug agencies. A drugs/youth worker is employed within the CDT to provide educational and preventative input to young people, and the CDT also offered a secondment to a student on the Youth Leadership Project.

There were a small number of other programmes provided under special funding initiatives. For example, in Overtown, the SRB funds a full-time drug prevention worker, delivering drug awareness in the community, to adults, parents and young people. In Hilltop, similarly, SRB had funded drug awareness work with Asian parents in response to local concerns.

Co-ordinated strategies

In her recent work on policing drug hotspots, Jacobson (1999) argues for multi-agency action that is:

- Based on careful examination of the parameters and nature of the problems, including consultation with residents and community groups.

- Multi-pronged (not just police enforcement).

- Sustained, but flexible to respond to changing patterns of behaviour among users and dealers.

- Sensitive to community relations.

Delivery of such an approach clearly demands good local knowledge, responsiveness to the local community, and mechanisms for co-ordinating the action of different agencies. As well as looking at specific interventions, we also examined the arrangements for ensuring such an approach to the drug markets in the study areas.

All of the areas were of course, covered by DATs, which were implementing a range of measures to improve treatment and access to treatment, and improve the relevance and coverage of drug education and prevention work. Examples from the study areas include:

- Implementing arrest referral schemes

- Implementing Drug Treatment and Testing Orders (DTTOs)

- Developing shared care arrangements

- Developing systems for monitoring treatment effectiveness

- Developing drug misuse good practice guidelines in relation to nightclubs

- Developing an employers' service to help with the development of drugs policies in the workplace

- First Aid training for injecting drug users

- Training on drug issues for youth and play workers

- Targeted education provision for pupils attending Pupil Referral Units

- Design and development of culturally appropriate drug education packages for black young people

- Running drug awareness days for schools and making sure that all secondary schools have a 'named teacher' responsible for drug education

However, DATs cover areas much bigger than neighbourhoods. Six of the eight DATs in the study covered whole cities (or local authority districts incorporating cities and their hinterlands), one the majority of a large county, and one a London Borough. Responding to the local nuances of neighbourhood drug markets, ensuring the right provision in each locality and making sure that the activities of different agencies at ground level are co-ordinated requires a more focused response.

For this reason, DATs are required to "develop an understanding of drug supply routes, markets and drug 'hotspots' within their areas" (DAT Annual Report Template Section 6). A number of possible actions are suggested, ranging from (at the highest level) 'jointly agreed action plans for market disruption based on needs analysis', to police action plans, and jointly agreed market analysis.

In none of the seven areas where the DAT was able to provide information to support the research did its co-ordinator have any detailed knowledge of the drug markets in the neighbourhoods we were studying. Their annual reports show that only one area, Beachville, had a jointly agreed market analysis. None had a jointly agreed action plan. Thus, the DATs in these areas were not developing detailed knowledge or co-ordinated responses at the neighbourhood level.

We also looked for multi-agency drug market strategies under the auspices of neighbourhood management or regeneration programmes.

As part of the Neighbourhood Renewal Strategy, the government is sponsoring pilot schemes for neighbourhood management, and encouraging the establishment of other similar schemes by local authorities. The priority for neighbourhood management is to tackle day-to-day quality of life issues by ensuring that public services are responsive to local problems and tackling them in a co-ordinated way. In areas with an active local drug market, neighbourhood management represents a good opportunity for co-ordinated and responsive action. At present, though, neighbourhood management structures are relatively unusual. Only one of the neighbourhoods in our study, Riverlands, had a neighbourhood manager, and this post was only recently established. Thus we were not able to discover the full contribution that this model could make to tackling an active and growing drug market. One initiative that was already proposed was to provide awareness training for front-line staff to support referral to and take up of drug services.

Area-based regeneration programmes represent the other major opportunity for the development of multi-agency strategies on single issues, as part of broader strategies for the regeneration of the neighbourhood as a whole. Six neighbourhoods in the study currently had area regeneration programmes. The Riverlands programme was funded by the local authority and applied only to one small estate of about 450 homes. The remaining programmes covered their neighbourhoods as a whole and were funded by the SRB, with between £7m and £26m SRB funding used as leverage in much bigger overall programmes over (typically) a seven-year period. One of the SRB neighbourhoods had also recently been awarded funding under the New Deal for Communities programme (NDC), operating over ten years and with NDC funding of approximately £50m. All of these programmes were managed by locally-based teams, had regular mechanisms for consulting the community, were responsible to multi-agency partnership boards and had working groups to implement specific aspects of their programme.

Three of the SRB programmes (and the planned NDC programme) were funding drug related projects. In Seaview, SRB funding had enabled the existing treatment service to target ethnic minority users. In Overtown, it paid for a Community Drug Prevention Worker (and the NDC promises to fund a drug and alcohol misusers support programme). In Hilltop, there were a number of projects: one working with Asian parents on drug issues, one researching low ethnic minority access to treatment, a drug education programme in schools, and a needle exchange project. Additionally, in Bankside, drug prevention initiatives were a core element of the role of the Community Intervention Officers funded by SRB.

This evidence suggests that area-based regeneration funding is used to support projects that tackle local drug markets. It seems to be used to fill service gaps and to tailor existing services to the specific needs of the locality. We did not find that any of the regeneration programmes were undertaking a strategic role in relation to drug markets – for example by funding research or development work or establishing multi-agency working groups.

Both of the neighbourhoods that did not have area-based regeneration programmes (Beachville and Kirkside East) were in the process of developing community forums and community plans, identifying local priorities to be addressed through mainstream services and funding bids. Kirkside East had a local co-ordinator and multi-agency panel for this purpose. In neither neighbourhood was 'tackling drugs' emerging as a priority issue.

6   Discussion

The extent, nature and impact of drug markets in deprived neighbourhoods

The eight neighbourhoods in this study were selected because they represented a broad cross-section of deprived neighbourhoods in England. No doubt there will be other deprived neighbourhoods where drug markets are more or less established, perhaps where there are no markets at all. The evidence from these eight neighbourhoods, however, is that heroin is very widely available, and that crack is now easily obtainable in most such places. The number of heroin users seems to be increasing and there are more sellers than there were in the mid-1990s. The number of crack users and sellers appears to be increasing even more rapidly. In a small number of areas, crack is now more commonly used than heroin and in others where it has become established it is as commonly used as heroin. In every case, we found a high degree of market separation between heroin and crack, on the one hand and other drugs. We focused on heroin and crack markets in this report. What can we conclude about these kinds of markets?

Firstly, that most of the selling in most markets takes place through a closed system. Deals are conducted by mobile telephone, with drugs exchanged at a convenient place, and delivered by runners. Central place markets tend to retain an open selling system in public places, to benefit from passing trade, and open street selling can also have a function when new drugs are being introduced, to establish the market and build a reputation and demand base. However, this is not the predominant form of selling.

Secondly, that there is a variety of distribution systems. Some markets are controlled by a small number of major operators, using middle level sellers and in some cases, small-scale sellers and runners. Other markets are more fluid, with a larger number of smaller independent operators. Violence is associated with drug dealing in both kinds of market, to enforce payment of debts, to resolve competition and to sanction informants, but extreme violence is found particularly in large, central place markets with contested distribution systems and buyers and sellers from outside the area as well as within it. It is in these kinds of markets, in particular, that levels of violence appear to be increasing.

Thirdly, that these characteristics of drug markets do vary by type of area. We found that markets in accessible inner city areas were more open to buyers and sellers; more likely to have buyers from outside the area; more likely to have open distribution arrangements and fixed site selling; and more likely to be exposed to competition than other areas. Outer city markets tended to have more stable buyer-seller arrangements. Drugs were often exchanged in public places but open street selling (i.e. casual trade with no introduction) was unusual in these markets.

The impact of drug markets on their host neighbourhoods also varies, and seems to be changing. The decline of open selling, with more and more deals conducted by mobile phone, is reducing nuisance associated with particular sites. Discarded needles are still a concern in some areas, in localised pockets, but in others appear to be less prevalent than they were. Levels of crime affecting residents are high, but burglary is declining. Thus, the reported increase in drug use does not appear to be resulting in increasing burglary in these areas. The impact of these developments is that an active drug market could be less disruptive to residents of a neighbourhood than it was several years ago. In some neighbourhoods where drug markets are vibrant, residents are not raising the issue as a priority for action because its impact is diminishing. On the other hand, residents of certain neighbourhoods are experiencing high levels of violence that make them acutely fearful of their personal safety, resulting in unwillingness to contribute evidence or get involved in activities that may help resolve the problems. Living in a climate of fear can restrict community cohesion and community action generally, not just in relation to drugs.

The drug market tends to be one of a number of neighbourhood problems, compounding other neighbourhood difficulties. We found no evidence that drug markets are a sufficient condition for neighbourhood decline or depopulation. However, where markets had become established, they were an impediment to regeneration, damaging community confidence and adding to the poor reputation of the area. Moreover, the market for crack, in particular, was providing a significant economic opportunity for young people whose formal labour market prospects were weak. It will be difficult to regenerate neighbourhoods without tackling drug markets.

Current responses and their impact

In the light of these findings, the responses of local agencies in the eight areas seem inadequate. We have not evaluated specific initiatives, and do not suggest that the interventions of local agencies were, in themselves, weak. Indeed, although some services were criticised locally for being insufficient or poorly targeted, others were well regarded, appropriate and responsive. However, in sum, the interventions were not containing the problem. Drug markets were growing. Their impact on their host neighbourhoods was changing, but in response to changes in drug market activity, not to agency interventions, and in some cases, neighbourhood impacts were worsening despite agency interventions.

It is clear that controlling the supply of illicit drugs and people's desire to use them is not entirely in the hands of local agencies. Many of the professionals we interviewed felt that they were responding to much bigger societal trends, trying to manage the problem locally, to limit the damage to individuals and communities. That said, our research does suggest that neighbourhood drug markets are not being as effectively managed as they might be, and points to some reasons why this is the case.

Knowledge about the drug market

Firstly, while individual agencies have specific knowledge, it appears that none of the multi-agency partnership groups that have the capacity to organise effective responses have detailed knowledge at the neighbourhood level about dealing arrangements, prices, availability of different drugs, levels of violence, or market trends. Disparate sources of information such as stop-and-search and drug arrest figures and treatment service referral data are not routinely brought together to generate neighbourhood profiles. The observations of front–line workers and residents are not routinely tapped to pick up changes in drug market activity, nor is the knowledge of drug users. Those who could be in a position to implement neighbourhood strategies have, therefore, no systematic way of identifying the problem they are supposed to tackle. Given that drug markets develop and evolve relatively quickly, this is a major obstacle.

Mechanisms for co-ordinated action

Secondly, the multi-agency mechanisms currently in place are not managing to deliver neighbourhood drugs strategies. Given their overview of services within the wider areas, DATs are the most obvious organisations to take responsibility for neighbourhood drugs strategies, tailoring broader strategies to local needs and filling gaps in provision. We are aware that in some other areas DATs are fulfilling this function. In the study areas, they were not. In only three of the areas were the DATs considered by most respondents to be effective – that is to say they were bodies that had commitment at strategic level from the relevant agencies, were 'more than just a talking shop' and were delivering useful action. Some faced operational difficulties. Two were still in the process of developing a strategy. One had suffered from the lack of a full-time co-ordinator and another was just becoming established after boundary changes. Given that DATs had been in existence for over five years at the time of this fieldwork, this is a disappointing picture. However, even the DATs that were considered effective had not developed a neighbourhood dimension to their work, apparently because of lack of capacity. Some of the DAT areas contained a number of neighbourhoods with vibrant drug markets.

Area regeneration programmes are another possible vehicle for the delivery of neighbourhood drugs strategies. In the neighbourhoods we studied, they were not fulfilling this function. There are a number of possible reasons. One is the inability of these programmes to respond to evolving problems. Most were initiated in the mid-1990s and their priorities, if not their exact spending programmes, were determined at that time. The evidence from the markets suggests rapid developments since then. Another possible reason is that programmes of this kind are usually geared to project spending, rather than to an ongoing strategic management role. While they provide the catalyst and the opportunity for ongoing multi-agency work, they do not function as multi-agency neighbourhood management boards, continuously monitoring and identifying problems and developing solutions. Some New Deal for Communities Programmes appear to be taking on a more strategic role, which may bring new opportunities. In Overtown, New Deal staff were meeting with the DAT co-ordinator to discuss how best to take forward their respective agenda in relation to the local drug market.

Multi-agency work around drug markets is, in any case, difficult to do well. The importance of community input in regeneration is increasingly emphasised (Social Exclusion Unit, 2001), but our case studies show that residents are often reluctant to take action against drug sellers for fear of reprisal. To compound the problem, some of the areas in which these markets are situated have complex community relations. Among our case studies, some were cohesive within two or three large ethnic groupings, but others were fragmented, with many small minority groups and cultures. Some inner city areas additionally had significant transient populations: people who were more loosely linked to the area and had weaker network ties. It is less easy for very diverse communities to come together to articulate the needs of the area, and more difficult for agencies to build lines of communication. More effort is needed to ensure culturally appropriate responses. In some areas, the main players in the drug market were from one or more minority groups, fuelling racial tensions and making responses very sensitive.

Regardless of area, tackling drugs together is problematic. Those working in the field (police and treatment agencies) often have conflicting perspectives. Other professionals whose work can contribute (such as housing managers and youth workers) may lack drug knowledge and the confidence to operate in multi-agency forums on the issue. And partnerships have to function in the face of a problem that seems to advance inexorably due to factors beyond local control. In his Wirral study, one of the few to look at this issue, Parker commented that the pace of change in the drug scene is such that professionals cannot rely on established positions, only on common sense, and that the failure of multi-agency responses to control the problem can result in people feeling de-skilled and disillusioned. "Heroin", he suggested "has in many ways deskilled these local decision makers." (Parker et al., 1998, p.148).

The absence of co-ordinated responses at neighbourhood level leaves individual agencies managing as best they can to deal with a growing problem. Our study suggests that responses are uneven and, in many cases, ineffective in relation to the scale of the problem. Why is this the case?

Enforcement

In relation to policing, our research suggests four main reasons why policing appears to have so little impact. There may well be others that did not emerge from these particular case studies.

The first is that the resources available are not proportionate to the scale of the problem. Beachville was the only area where the market appeared to be of a manageable scale. It was a small market, in a geographically isolated area, and not surrounded by multiple drug markets with similar problems. In other areas, the markets were bigger. The sheer numbers of people operating at a low level, as dealers and runners, made it difficult to keep on top of the problem in any sustained way. Street dealers who were arrested were simply replaced by others. Large urban areas not only had large markets but several of them. The ability to focus consistently on one area was limited. In Seaview, East-Docks and Kirkside East, limited enforcement activity was attributed by police respondents to the fact that resources were channelled toward more significant markets nearby. Drug markets, are of course, not the only call on police resources in these areas. As one officer commented, any problem can be tackled with sufficient resources, but the need to spread the resources around a number of problems means that none can have sustained attention.

> "If you resource a problem for long enough you can tackle the problem and then somebody else's problem becomes a priority and all the resources go to that problem, and all of a sudden it starts to come back on you. We have got to look at the geographics, what attracts these people [drug dealers]." (Police officer – Seaview)

The distribution of resources is guided by the need to achieve performance targets. Some officers felt that local performance targets for drug offences were easier to achieve than those for burglary, robbery and car crime. It was difficult to justify resources to exceeding drug targets, when targets in other areas of policing were in danger of being under-achieved.

Second, markets had adapted in response to police tactics, and the range of effective police responses had become more limited. The reduction in street selling and the requirement for new buyers to consume drugs on site are two examples.

Third, police were operating in an environment of low public confidence. Police and residents in most areas acknowledged relatively poor police/community relations. Residents demonstrated a reluctance to trust, an unwillingness to engage with and a level of dissatisfaction with the performance of the police. For example, a report for the SRB in East-Docks stated that many residents were discouraged by a lack of police presence in the area. It questioned the police's commitment to East-Docks and described them as 'generally ineffective'. A local agency professional complained about the loss of the local community officer who had spent five years establishing contacts and trust in the neighbourhood. Similarly, in Hilltop, one agency professional noted:

> "...there are no foot patrols anymore, they don't tend to prevent crime by moving people on. It feels like Hilltop has been given up on, but I don't think it has." (Drug worker – Hilltop)

Poor police/community relations limited the supply of information from the community to the police. Moreover, in several of the inner city areas with multi-ethnic communities, officers commented that the need to build better relations with the community, after a long period of discontent, had limited the extent of their enforcement activity. Drug sellers from ethnic minorities dominated the two main open markets in Seaview and Bankside. The local inspector in Seaview recognised that previously the market had been placed in "the 'too-hard-to-police' basket", which was partly responsible for growth in activity in the market. Similar concerns were noted in Bankside:

> "[The police are] too frightened to deal with the issues as they relate to Asian or Black people." (Agency professional – Bankside)

These concerns had apparently been exacerbated by the implications of the Stephen Lawrence Inquiry Report (Macpherson, 1999) alongside a degree of critical media coverage that has highlighted the issue of policing race.

In combination, these difficulties make the policing of urban drug markets seem, at times, a demanding task. Civil enforcement measures have helped little. Local authorities are understandably reluctant to evict tenants who they may ultimately have to re-house elsewhere, and the gathering of evidence for possession proceedings and for ASBOs is time-consuming and often runs up against the reluctance of neighbours to provide it. Professional witnesses are expensive. Although these measures are occasionally invoked in severe cases of anti-social behaviour, cases where drug selling is involved are usually treated as a criminal rather than a civil matter.

Treatment provision

Many of the treatment services in and around our neighbourhood markets were having some impact on drug users' lives. However, we identified a number of factors that were inhibiting their potential to reach more drug users and have a greater impact.

Similar to enforcement strategies, treatment provision in all of the markets studied was under-resourced given the size of the drug-using population. Many treatment providers reported that the scope and range of the interventions they offered was curtailed by cash or staffing limitations (despite a recent injection of additional resources from central government). While some were able to provide specialist services, they were not able to meet the needs of the different types of drug users. Others were able to offer a broad range of interventions to a limited number of clients. Several of the services we visited had waiting lists.

There appears to be little attention paid to where services are located and what types of services are offered within an area. Obviously, there will always be a limit on what services can be sited within a locality. However, currently the decision-making processes about what should be provided and where a service is located seem haphazard. When new services are developed or existing services extended, they tend to be located with established services and not necessarily where the potential client group is. This is likely to make the service less attractive to those who have to travel to receive help. Indeed, a point made by several of those working in services was that many clients would be unprepared to travel more than two miles in order to participate in services. Some of the services we visited either had little knowledge of changing drug use patterns within their area or were not responding to the changing needs of the local drug users. This resulted in a mismatch between the type of service provided and the problems experienced locally. For example, in one area researchers were told by a service that crack use was not common and therefore they did not offer services for this group. However, the researchers were able to speak to a number of drug users who were using crack and they indicated they knew many other crack users within the area. Such users reported that they did not attend the service because there was nothing on offer to them.

Some of the pressures on drug treatment services could be reduced if GPs were more involved in the care of drug users. In all areas, there was the obvious potential of involving GPs in the provision of drug treatment, although this was rarely realised. There were some good examples of shared care between drug services and GPs and once such schemes were established, they appeared to work well. Services we spoke with had tried for many years to convince GPs to work with them but most were resistant. GPs are still reluctant to work with drug users, whom they see as a difficult and troublesome group.

Most drug users identified that treatment services in the eight areas involved were generally unresponsive to their needs. Waiting lists for methadone treatment were a particular concern. Services (DDUs in particular) were reported as not responding to individual circumstances (for example, it is difficult for sex workers to attend DDUs in normal opening hours). However, unless services are more flexible they are unlikely to retain those who have the most chaotic and problematic lifestyles.

Across all sites, there was a lack of specialist services for crack users. This is of particularly concern given the recent and emergent development of crack markets in all sites apart from one. Some treatment services were aware of this development and were initiating new work, but most had little idea of the scale of the problem they faced. This has implications on a number of levels. Unless services have an idea of market changes, they are unlikely to respond appropriately. Services therefore need to know their market. Market knowledge is particularly important to services to enable them to lobby for funds enabling them to respond to emerging and developing problems.

Generally, we found that the needs of particular groups of drug users were not being catered for. We found some good examples of specialist services for young people but they were poorly served at mainstream services. Most services seemed to have attempted to engage with women but they were still under-represented at services. Drug users from ethnic minority groups in some of our sites made-up a large minority of users – again this group was generally under-represented at services given the numbers of local users. A number of reasons were identified for the lack of engagement with these groups. Generally, services were seen as unresponsive to their specific needs. In particular, concerns were expressed about confidentiality – for young people and those from specific ethnic groups these concerns revolved around family and friends being made aware of their drug problem and for women it was related to children. Make-up of staff teams was also a concern.

Outreach would appear to be a useful device in aiding the process of engagement with these groups by services. By building up a relationship with users outside the formal service setting outreach staff may be able to encourage users into treatment. Such workers would also be able to gather information about local drug trends and how the market is developing.

Given the points raised above, it is difficult to see how drug services could look beyond dealing with the drug treatment needs of their clients to also consider their housing, education, training and employment needs. However, unless these issues are also tackled then the likelihood of success in treatment and movement away from a drug using 'lifestyle' is potentially limited. This is particularly the case in the markets that we studied because of the limited opportunities that exist.

Education/prevention

In the areas studied, we found that drug education is being delivered widely in secondary schools and in the majority of primary schools. However, we also found that it is not usually accredited in line with new national standards, nor is it usually designed in response to local market conditions or developed as part of a local drug prevention strategy involving youth and community groups and specialist programmes for young people particularly at risk. The lack of local strategies is an obvious reason, but there are others, principally that education and prevention activities (and the treatment of young users early in their drug-using careers) are falling to a number of organisations, none of which sees it as their primary responsibility.

One respondent particularly commented on the difficulty of delivering a co-ordinated programme reaching young users or potential users.

"The young person is the weakest strand (in the drugs policy). Drugs education is difficult for schools to deliver. There is reluctance because they believe their image will be tainted if they start making drugs an issue. Educational welfare has only just taken a post, the youth service doesn't do anything and 14- to 16-year-olds are excluded from Drug Treatment and Testing Orders. There is little in place to pick up on the young user." (Police Superintendent and member of DAT – Kirkside East)

Since all the agencies concerned have other responsibilities and pressures, drug issues can assume low priority. For example, a co-ordinator for NHSS suggested that the failure of most schools to develop an accredited drug education programme was probably due to shortages of trained teachers and the decision to prioritise other aspects of the NHSS scheme (such as healthy eating) that are easier for them to tackle or seen as more advantageous to the reputation of the school. Some agencies may also be reluctant to play a more proactive role in preventing drug use or educating potential users. Several of the youth workers we spoke to believed that it was inappropriate for youth workers to be associated with an anti-drugs message, preferring to make information available to young people but to respect their choices. If effective programmes are to be delivered locally, the contributions that can be made by different agencies clearly need to be actively negotiated, not passively assumed.

7   Recommendations

There is no doubt that dealing with local drug markets is a difficult task, and that local actions will form only one element of the solution. However, our report paints a gloomy picture of interventions to date. We suggest that there is room for improvement at local level, and that the impact of drug markets on their host neighbourhoods could be significantly reduced by better co-ordinated, better resourced, and better targeted approaches.

The government's strategy for Neighbourhood Renewal reflects a widely held belief, based on 30 years of urban policy experimentation, that neighbourhoods with concentrated problems benefit from a local focus: a co-ordinated multi-agency approach that can identify and prioritise specific local problems, draw on local knowledge, forge partnerships between workers at ground level and link neighbourhood strategies to wider mainstream strategies and funding streams. These advantages of a neighbourhood focus certainly apply to drug market activity. So how can tackling local drug markets become a more integral part of the neighbourhood renewal agenda?

Neighbourhood drugs strategies in NDC areas

Our first suggestion is that regeneration partnerships in NDC areas should be required to review drug market activity and to develop an appropriate strategy, if one is needed. Areas designated for NDC funding have the opportunity to develop wide-ranging regeneration programmes with the genuine involvement of the community and local agencies. The opportunity to tackle drug markets as part of these programmes should not be missed. NDC partnerships should develop task groups with appropriate representation and knowledge to take forward their drug market strategies.

These strategies should have four main pillars:

- Ground-level responses to enforce the law and curtail violence, disorder and nuisance associated with drug selling.

- Measures to develop community confidence, raise awareness and support communities in addressing the problem.

- Locally available services for drug users that are appropriate and accessible.

- Co-ordinated prevention and education strategies so that young people who are exposed to drug market activity have relevant information and support with which to make decisions.

The measures that will be appropriate will vary locally, and we are not proposing a blueprint to be imposed on every neighbourhood. Figure 7.1 illustrates the kinds of measures (drawn from this research and other research and practice) that might be explored by local partnerships.

The evidence of the neighbourhoods in this study suggests that local strategies should certainly contain clear mechanisms for keeping information about drug market developments up-to-date (involving drug users in this process), as well as public relations strategies designed to limit the labelling of neighbourhoods as drug markets.

The role of DATs

Outside the NDC areas, regeneration partnerships may be more limited in their funding and scope, or there may be active drug market areas with no regeneration partnership. In these cases, DATs or CDRPs will need to take the initiative in developing similar local strategies. They will also want to work closely with partners in the NDC areas, building awareness of drug issues and, through information and training, developing the capacity of decision-makers in these organisations to tackle local drug markets confidently and appropriately as part of their neighbourhood renewal programmes.

DATs are already required to develop an understanding of drug hotspots in their areas. They should be required to list these hotspots and to identify which have a neighbourhood drugs strategy in place. DATs should thus be accountable for the development of neighbourhood drugs strategies, either directly or through regeneration partnerships.

It is not clear that, at present, DATs have the capacity to support the development of neighbourhood drugs strategies, and we recommend that this situation is reviewed. DATs need to be equipped to fulfil this function, perhaps through the appointment of neighbourhood support workers.

Figure 7.1: *Measures that might be included in neighbourhood drugs strategies*

Ground-level responses to enforce the law and curtail violence, disorder and nuisance associated with drug selling, including:

- Local policing strategies agreed with the local community, and that are proactive, based on well-structured intelligence at all levels, and involve a significant visible street presence.

- Close liaison and information-sharing protocols between police and housing departments.

- Security measures for empty properties and other specific situational measures.

Measures to develop community confidence, raise awareness and support communities in addressing the problem, including:

- Drug awareness programmes, support groups for families of users, anonymous 'drug watch' schemes, police protection and professional witness schemes. Community capacity-building generally may be an essential pre-requisite of these strategies.

- Encouragement of local people and staff to report discarded needles, clear reporting systems and service agreements for prompt needle clear-up.

- Systems to protect drug users from violence and to increase the flow of information to police (such as the 'Ugly Mugs' scheme used in some sex work sites), and to engage drug users as part of the local community.

Locally available services for drug users that are appropriate and accessible, including:

- Generic local services.

- Methadone prescribing by GPs.

- specialist services, relevant to local circumstances and with attention to the needs of ethnic minority communities.

- Hepatitis C screening , in conjunction with pre- and post-test counselling.

- Support for users coming out of treatment (for example, training or housing support).

- Active targeting of crack users by treatment agencies.

- Proactive and targeted outreach work and needle exchange.

Co-ordinated prevention and education strategies so that young people who are exposed to drug market activity have relevant information and support with which to make decisions, including:

- Training for non-specialist staff (e.g. housing staff, neighbourhood wardens, youth worker) in drug awareness and service provision.

- Intensive intervention programmes with young people at risk of becoming heavily involved in drug use or selling.

- Education strategies that conform to national standards and which are tailored to local drug market conditions.

Resources for neighbourhood drugs strategies

Our report suggests that there are genuine resource problems hindering the delivery of effective local action to combat drug markets, particularly concerning law enforcement. However, we are not in a position to determine the level of resources needed. Nor is it clear what return could be expected from higher levels of investment at local level. This needs to be explored further. We suggest that pilot sites for the development of neighbourhood drugs strategies should be identified (possibly under the New Deal for Communities Initiative). Resources should be made available to these areas in response to local need as identified by multi-agency partnerships and appropriate government departments. Local flexibility should also be given to remove institutional disincentives to performance (such as performance indicators) where necessary, and to keep on top of fast-moving developments, by freeing up money for tackling drug markets from other programme areas or reserving unallocated funds. The cost and effectiveness of these strategies should be fully evaluated in comparison with control areas with similar drug markets.

Meanwhile, the Communities Against Drugs (CAD) Initiative represents an opportunity to develop co-ordinated local approaches. £220 million is being given to CDRPs to tackle drug-related crime in high crime areas with significant drug problems over the next three years. The aim is to focus on local priorities with partnerships deciding how the monies should be spent. The boroughs containing our study areas have received between £100,000 and £900,000 under this initiative; a large amount if targeted to selected neighbourhoods, but not if spread thinly. We therefore recommend that CDRPs invest a small amount of money in mapping drug markets and getting up-to-date information on market conditions and developments, before determining their spending programmes.

Finally, we acknowledge that effective action against heroin and crack will not be resolved by interventions only at local level. It requires adequate resourcing at national and international level as well as critical thinking about appropriate and differentiated strategies for dealing with the different challenges of heroin and crack. This report reveals a complex and growing problem that requires a concerted and co-ordinated response at all levels.

References

Akhtar, S. and South, N. (2000) 'Hidden from heroin's history: Heroin use and dealing within an English Asian community – a case study', in Natarajan, M. and Hough, M. (eds) *Illegal Drug Markets: from research to prevention policy*. New York: Crime Prevention Studies Vol. 11.

Beebe, J. (1995) 'Basic concepts and techniques of rapid appraisal', *Human organization*, 54 (1): 42-51.

Bennett, T. (1998) *Drugs and Crime: the results of research on drug testing and interviewing arrestees*. London: Home Office.

Bennett, T. (2000) *Drugs and Crime: the results of the second developmental stage of the NEW-ADAM programme*. Home Office Research Study 205. London: Home Office.

Bottoms, A.E. and Wiles, P. (1986), 'Housing Tenure and Residential Community Crime Careers in Britain', in Reiss, A.J. and Tonry, M. (eds) '*Communities and Crime*'. Chicago: University of Chicago Press.

Bottoms, A, Mawby, R.I and Xanthos, P. (1989) 'A Tale of Two Estates', in Downes, D. (ed) *Crime and the City*. London: MacMillan.

Bourgois, P. (1995) *In Search of Respect: Selling Crack in El Barrio*. Cambridge: Cambridge University Press.

Brain, K., Parker, H. and Bottomley, T. (1998) *Evolving Crack Cocaine Careers: new users, quitters and long term combination drug users in N.W. England*. Occasional Paper. London: Home Office.

Burr, A. (1987). 'Chasing the Dragon. Heroin Misuse, Delinquency and Crime in the Context of South London Culture', *British Journal of Criminology*, 27(4): 333-357.

Chatterton, M., Varley, M. and Longmead-Jones, P. (1998). *Testing Performance Indicators for Local Anti-Drug Strategies*. Police Research Series Paper 97. London: Home Office.

DETR (2000) *Measuring Multiple Deprivation at the Small Area Level: the indices of deprivation 2000*. London: DETR.

DfEE (1998) *Protecting Young People: good practice in drug education in schools and the youth service*. London: DfEE.

Dorn, N., James, D. and South, N. (1987) *The Limits of Informal Surveillance – Four Case Studies in Identifying Neighbourhood Heroin Problems*. London: Institute for the Study of Drug Dependency.

Dorn, N., Murji, K., and South, N. (1992) *Traffickers: Drug Markets and Law Enforcement*. London: Routledge.

Duke, K., McGregor, S. and Smith, L. (1995). *Activating Local Networks: a comparison of two community development approaches to drug prevention*. DPI Paper 10. London: Home Office.

Eck, J. (1995) 'A General Model of the Geography of Illicit Retail Markets' in Eck, J.E. and Weisburd, D. (eds) *Crime and Place*. New York: Criminal Justice Press.

Edmunds, M., Hough, M. and Urquia, M. (1996) *Tackling Local Drug Markets*. Crime Detection and Prevention Series Paper No. 80. London: Home Office.

Edmunds, M., May, T., Hough, M. and Hearnden, I. (1998) *Arrest Referral: Emerging Lessons from Research*. DPI Paper 23. London: Home Office.

Edmunds, M., Hough, M. and Turnbull, P. (1999) *Doing Justice to Treatment: referring offenders to drug services*. DPAS Paper 2. London: Home Office.

Fagan, J. (1989). 'The Social Organisation of Drug Use and Drug Dealing Among Urban Gangs', *Criminology*, 27(4): 633-67.

Forsyth, A., Hammersley, R., Lavelle, T. and Murray, K. (1992) 'Geographical Aspects of Scoring Illicit Drugs', *British Journal of Criminology*, 32(3): 292-309.

Glennerster, H., Lupton, R., Noden, P., and Power, A. (1998) *Poverty, Social Exclusion and Neighbourhood: studying the area bases of social exclusion*. CASEpaper 22. London: CASE.

Graham, J. (2000) *Drug Markets and Neighbourhood Regeneration* (unpublished report – CASE, LSE).

Hayes, G. and Baker, O. (1998) *Drug Prevalence in the UK: Update 1998: report to the Department Of Health*. London: DOH.

Haynes, P. (1998) 'Drug-using Offenders in South London: trends and outcomes' *Journal of Substance Abuse Treatment*, 15(5): 449-456.

Haynes, G., Bottomley, T. and Gray, A. (2000) *National Crack Cocaine Treatment and Response Strategy: minimum and maximum requirements for effective practice and service development*. Department of Health Advisory Document to the UKADCU.

Henderson, P. (1995) *Drugs Prevention and Community Development: Principles of Good Practice*. DPI Paper 7. London: Home Office.

HM Government (1995) *Tackling Drugs Together: a strategy for England 1995-1998*. London: HMSO.

HM Government (1998) *Tackling Drugs To Build A Better Britain*. London: HMSO.

Hobbs, D. (1995) *Bad Business: professional crime in modern Britain*. Oxford: Oxford University Press.

Home Office (1999) *Evaluating Effectiveness: drugs prevention research conference*. DPI Paper 20. London: Home Office.

Howard, R., Beadle, P. and Maitland, J. (1993) *Across the Divide: building community partnerships to tackle drug misuse*. London: Department of Health.

Hurry, J. and Lloyd, C. (1997) *A follow-up evaluation of Project Charlie: a life skills drug education programme for primary schools*. Drug Prevention Initiative Paper 16. London: Home Office.

Jacobson, J. (1999) *Policing Drug Hot-Spots*. Police Research Series Paper 109. London: Home Office.

Johnson, B., Williams, T., Kojo, A. and Sanabria, H. (1990) 'Drug Abuse in the Inner City: Impact on Hard Drug Users and the Community', in Tonry, M. and Wilson, J.Q. (eds) *Drugs and Crime*. Chicago: University of Chicago Press.

Johnson, M. and Carroll, M. (1995) *Dealing with Diversity: good practice in drug prevention work with racially and culturally diverse communities*. London: Home Office.

Lee, M. (1996) 'London: "Community damage limitation" through policing?' in Dorn, N., Jepson, J. and Savona, E. (eds) *European Drug Policy and Enforcement*. Basingstoke: Macmillan.

Lee, P. and Murie, A. (1997) *Poverty, Housing Tenure and Social Exclusion*. York: Joseph Rowntree Foundation.

Lloyd, C. and Griffiths, P. (1998) 'Editorial: Problems for the Future? Drug use among vulnerable groups of young people', *Drugs: Education, Prevention and Policy*, 5(3): 213-216.

Lupton, R. (2001) *Places Apart? The initial report of CASE's areas study*. CASEreport14, London: CASE.

Macpherson, W. (1999) *The Stephen Lawrence Inquiry: report of an inquiry by Sir William Macpherson of Cluny*. London: HMSO.

May, T., Hough, M. and Edmunds, M. (2000) 'Sex Markets and Drug Markets: Examining the Links', *Crime Prevention and Community Safety: an International Journal*, 2(2): 25-41.

May, T., Haracopos, A., Turnbull, P.J. and Hough, M. (2000) *Serving Up: the impact of low-level police enforcement on drug markets*. Police Research Series Paper 133. London: Home Office.

May, T., Edmunds, M. and Hough, M. (1999) *Street Business: the links between sex and drug markets*. Police Research Series Paper 118. London: Home Office.

Murji, K. (1998) *Policing Drugs*. Hampshire: Ashgate.

Natarajan, M., Clarke, R. and Johnson, B.D. (1995) 'Telephones as facilitators of drug dealing: a research agenda', *European Journal of Criminal Policy and Research*, 3(3): 137-154.

Newburn, T. and Elliott, J. (1998) *Police Anti-Drugs Strategies: tackling drugs together three years on*. Crime Detection and Prevention Series Paper 89. London: Home Office.

Page, D. (2000) *Communities in the Balance: the reality of social exclusion on housing estates.* York: Joseph Rowntree Foundation.

Parker, H., Bakx, K., and Newcombe, R. (1988) *Living with Heroin: the impact of a drugs 'epidemic' on an English community.* Milton Keynes: Open University Press.

Parker, H., and Newcombe, R. (1987) 'Heroin Use and Acquisitive Crime in an English Community', *Sociology*, 38(3): 331-350.

Parker, H. and Bottomley, T. (1996) *Crack Cocaine and Drug-Crime Careers.* London: Home Office.

Parker, H., Bury, C. and Egginton, R. (1998) *New Heroin Outbreaks among Young People in England and Wales.* Crime Prevention and Detection Paper 92. London: Home Office.

Pearson G., Gilman, M. and McIver, S. (1985) *Young People and Heroin: an examination of heroin use in the north of England.* Health Education Council Research Report No.8.

Pearson, G. and Gilman, M. (1994) 'Local and regional variations in drug misuse: the British heroin epidemic of the 1980s', in Strang, J. and Gossop, M. (eds) *Heroin Addiction and Drug Policy: the British System.* Oxford: Oxford Medical Publications.

Plant, M. and Miller, P. (2000) 'Drug use has declined among teenagers in the UK', *British Medical Journal*, 320: 1536 (3 June).

Power, A. and Bergin, E. (1999) *Neighbourhood Management.* CASEpaper 31. London: CASE.

Ramsay, M. and Partridge, S. (1998) *Drug Misuse Declared in 1998: results from the British Crime Survey.* Home Office Research Study 197. London: Home Office.

Ruggiero, V. and South, N. (1995) *Eurodrugs, drug use, markets and trafficking in Europe.* London: UCL Press.

Social Exclusion Unit (2001) *A New Commitment to Neighbourhood Renewal: national strategy action plan.* London: Cabinet Office.

Turnbull, P. J., McSweeney, T., Webster, R., Edmunds, M. and Hough, M. (2000) *Drug Treatment and Testing Orders: evaluation report.* Home Office Research Study 212. London: Home Office.

Ward, J. and Rhodes, J. (2001) *Drugs Prevention through Youth Work*. DPAS Briefing Paper 12. London: Home Office.

Weisburd, D. and Green, L. (1998) 'Policing Drug Hot Spots: The Jersey City Drug Market Analysis Experiment' in Bayley D. H. (ed) *What Works in Policing*. New York: Oxford University Press.

Wood, W. and Vamplew, C. (1999) *Neighbourhood Images in Teesside, Regeneration or Decline?* York: Joseph Rowntree Foundation.

Wright, A., Waymount, A. and Gregory, F. (1993) *Drug Squads: drug law enforcement and intelligence in England and Wales*. London: Police Foundation.

Glossary of terms

- ASBO: Anti-Social Behaviour Order. Court order to curb anti-social behaviour.

- Central place market: long-established with wide reputations, drawing in buyers from outside the area. These markets had some degree of 'open-ness' to casual buyers, some street dealing and 'closed' trade. Prone to competition.

- CARAT: Counselling, Assessment, Referral, Advice and Throughcare.

- CASE: Centre for the Analysis of Social Exclusion.

- Closed market: access to the market is limited to known and trusted participants. An unknown buyer needs someone to introduce them or vouch for them before they can make a purchase.

- CDRP: Crime and Disorder Reduction Partnership.

- CDT: Community Drug Team.

- DAT: Drug Action Team. Multi-agency partnership to tackle drugs at local or health authority level.

- DDU: Drug Dependency Unit.

- Dealer: someone who buys and sells drugs.

- Deals: the process of buying and selling drugs.

- Deprived neighbourhood: an area among the 10 per cent most deprived in the country based on six domains: income, employment, health and disability, skills and training, housing and access to services.

- DRG: Drug Reference Group.

- DTTO: Drug Treatment and Testing Order. Court order obliging offender to undergo drug treatment and testing.

- High level dealer: Seller who is involved in direct importation or purchase of large amounts of drugs, selling on to a few dealers lower down the distribution chain.

- IMD: Index of Multiple Deprivation.

- Local market: most buyers are local, with firmly established buyer/seller relationships. Well established and stable.

- Middle level dealer: Seller who works between the high level dealers and those who sell directly to the market.

- NDC: New Deal for Communities. Area-based regeneration programme.

- Neighbourhood: relatively small area made up of several thousand people, delineated within physical boundaries where people identify their home and where they live out their private lives.

- NHSS: National Healthy Schools Standard.

- Open market: A market where there are no barriers to access. Buyers can purchase drugs without being known or introduced to a dealer.

- Poly drug user: Users who use a range of different drugs.

- Runner: Someone who delivers drugs to users on behalf of sellers.

- SRB: Single Regeneration Budget. Area-based regeneration programme.

- UKADCU: United Kingdom Anti-Drugs Co-ordination Unit.

- User/dealer: Sellers who finance their own drug use by buying drugs for others, thereby reducing the cost of their own use.

Appendix 1   Summary of area-based policies

National Neighbourhood Renewal Strategy	A new approach, rather than a specific programme. Covers programmes under many government departments. Key elements: • Minimum targets below which no neighbourhood should fall (e.g. crime, educational standards). • Specific targets to raise standards in worst off areas (e.g. DfEE targets to raise employment rates in 30 areas with weakest labour market position). • Local Strategic Partnerships, which will be expected to develop neighbourhood renewal strategies. • Community involvement, Community Empowerment Fund and Community Chests.
Neighbourhood Management	Initially a pilot programme to test benefits of putting a single neighbourhood manager (or team) in charge of an area to be a focus for local concerns, to develop service agreements, or to manage devolved budgets
Neighbourhood Wardens and Street Wardens Programme	Government programme to give grants and support to areas wanting to establish warden schemes. Wardens are a uniformed, semi-official presence designed to assist with environmental improvements, housing management and community development
Neighbourhood Renewal Fund	Government Fund to improve public services in the most deprived parts of the most deprived local authorities
New Deal for Communities	Area regeneration programme for 39 areas so far – all relatively small areas of approximately 4000 households. Programmes designed and implemented by local partnerships, with communities in the lead. Funding of £20m-£50m over a ten-year period to tackle worklessness and poor prospects, improving health, tackling crime, raising educational achievement and improving housing and the physical environment.
Health Action Zones	Twenty-six zones covering wider areas, typically the size of a health authority. New approach to public health linking health with regeneration, employment, education, housing and anti-poverty initiatives.

Notes: There are other area-based policies including Employment Zones, Surestart and Education Action Zones. These are less relevant to the drugs agenda and have not been included here.

Appendix 2

Respondents interviewed in each area (excluding drug users)

Neighbourhood	Housing	Police	Drug workers	Probation/YOT	GPs	Youth and Community	Regeneration	Residents (incl young people)	Other	TOTAL
Seaview	2	7	10	2	1	2	0	10	1	35
Bankside	3	4	5	2	1	0	5	8	4	32
Riverlands	2	4	10	4	2	4	1	13	7	47
Hilltop	4	11	5	1	2	3	0	10	1	37
East-Docks	2	1	4	1	1	4	1	10	4	28
Kirkside East	4	2	17	3	0	8	1	14	11	60
Overtown	2	2	6	2	0	0	2	31	7	52
Beachville	0	2	7	1	0	3	1	17	5	36
TOTAL	19	33	64	16	7	24	11	113	40	327

Note: 'Drug workers' includes staff of treatment agencies, needle exchange, specific drug projects (e.g. awareness projects), arrest referral workers, outreach workers, and DAT representatives.

RDS Publications

Requests for Publications

Copies of our publications and a list of those currently available may be obtained from:

Home Office
Research, Development and Statistics Directorate
Communication Development Unit
Room 275, Home Office
50 Queen Anne's Gate
London SW1H 9AT
Telephone: 020 7273 2084 (answerphone outside of office hours)
Facsimile: 020 7222 0211
E-mail: publications.rds@homeoffice.gsi.gov.uk

alternatively

why not visit the RDS web-site at

Internet: http://www.homeoffice.gov.uk/rds/index.htm

where many of our publications are available to be read on screen or downloaded for printing.